A
Time
for
Comfort

Marie D. Jones, Anne Broyles,
Rebecca Christian, June Eaton,
Susan Farr Fahncke, Carol Smith,
Natalie Walker Whitlock

 Publications International, Ltd.

Contents

Hope Heals

*Now may our Lord Jesus Christ
himself and God our Father, who
loved us and through grace gave us
eternal comfort and good hope, comfort your hearts and strengthen them
in every good work and word.*

2 Thessalonians 2:16–17

THE SIGN OF THREE

The day Cheryl's daughter was admitted to the hospital was like any other in
Southern California. The weather was
mild, and the sun was out, with only a few
fluffy clouds in the deep blue sky. As other
children played outside, Cheryl stood with
her knees shaking as the doctor told her
that her six-year-old daughter, Anna, was
hovering between life and death.

The doctor explained that Anna had suffered an aneurysm, a burst blood vessel in the brain, and that the situation was deeply serious. His words took Cheryl's breath away.

With her husband off on military duty, Cheryl felt so alone in her suffering. Her family was several states away, and though they were rushing to be with her, Cheryl wished Jack could be there. He was in a wartime situation, and she could not even reach him until things settled in the region where he was stationed. For now, she would have to go it alone . . . at least until her mother and brother arrived.

A helpful neighbor collected Cheryl's clothes and toiletries from home while Cheryl stayed with Anna in the hospital as she recovered from emergency surgery to drain the blood. Some of the blood was still on her brain, and it was touch and go. Cheryl spent hours holding Anna's hand, praying to God that he would spare her child. She felt as though her whole life was in a state of suspended animation.

When her family arrived, they helped tremendously, and Cheryl didn't feel quite so alone. She still wished Jack could get home but knew it was out of his hands. Cheryl's mom was a great help, even encouraging Cheryl to go home and rest awhile, but she refused. She did not want to leave Anna's side for one moment. She just didn't know if that one moment would be their last together. . . .

Only when is it dark enough can you see the stars.

That night, Anna took a turn for the worse. The blood had pooled in her brain and was causing swelling. The doctor would have to perform another surgery. There was nothing Cheryl could do but have faith in the surgeons and in God.

The surgery took several hours. Cheryl's chest pounded, and her head ached. She had not eaten in 14 hours and could not keep anything down. She was sleep-deprived, terrified, and longed for word from Jack. As she waited with her family, she got the sudden urge to be alone and went outside for a walk.

The night was mild and clear, with stars piercing the black velvet blanket of sky. Cheryl closed her eyes and prayed that God would give her more time with Anna. She also prayed that Jack would come home soon, to a happy reunion.

When she opened her eyes, something made her look upward. Not one, but three shooting stars streaked across the sky in unison, and Cheryl felt her heart leap into her throat at the sight. Tears filled her eyes as she let out a huge sigh and then took in a deep, hearty breath, filling her lungs with nourishing oxygen.

"Thank you for the sign," she whispered, sure that the three shooting stars were her, Anna, and Jack, and that God had been trying to tell her they would all be together soon.

Cheryl went back inside, where her brother was looking for her. He told her excitedly that not only had Anna pulled through the surgery and was doing well, but that Jack had called Cheryl's cell phone. He was coming home...in three days.

Lord, give me a sign that you are watching over me and mine tonight. Show me a miracle, send me an angel. I know that I must have faith to see your grace at work, but sometimes my faith is shaky and I have doubts and fears. In those times, come to me in a way that I will know you. Give me a sign, dear Lord, and the wisdom to recognize it when I see it. Amen.

THE LIGHTHOUSE

Hope is our anchor in the storm,
Our comfort in the night.
Love is the beacon that directs us
As we move toward the light.

In the randomness of life, when the good that you, O God, will and want for me isn't possible and trouble and loss overtake me, it is enough to know that you are already there with comfort, support, inspiration, and arms to hold me. I can bear anything if you take the steps forward with me.

Our help is in the name of the Lord, who made heaven and earth.

Psalm 124:8

Blessed be God, because he has not rejected my prayer or removed his steadfast love from me.

Psalm 66:20

Ponder possible reasons God might have had for sending an ordinary star—one among millions that so easily could've been lost in the cosmos—as a signal to announce Jesus' birth. And then if that wasn't enough, why use this star as a guide? Think of it as a present-day reminder to look up, not down. Look for the unexpected and count on God to fulfill the promise for changes to take place. Counting on a gentler, calmer tomorrow places an entire garden of stars like daffodils in the cold winter sky.

When doubt fills my mind, when my heart is in turmoil, quiet me and guide me, renewed in hope and cheer.

Psalm 94:19 TLB

LOSING TO WIN

Farron had worked for the accounting firm for more than 12 years. But her loyalty and dedication didn't stop the company from laying her off at the first sign of lower-than-usual profits. With only two weeks of severance and a wish for luck, her employers sent her off into the unknown world of unemployment.

It took her days to get over her anger and feelings of betrayal. She was bolstered only by the phone calls she received from two of her coworkers, who had also been given the unceremonious boot.

Although she usually wasn't one to pray, Farron couldn't help giving it a try one night, alone in bed with her own anxiety. She prayed for the strength to get through this rough period, but most of all, she prayed for a little guidance on what new direction her life could take.

All she had ever done was accounting work, and she was not sure if the workplace had much need for her, especially in such tough economic times. How she would find a salary comparable to her last was beyond her. She had a mortgage and a car payment and a lot of credit card debt from living high on the hog and thinking she would always have a job to pay for it.

> *Be as the water lily, which—when faced with thick and muddied waters—rises through the darkness with hope, determination, and courage to break the surface and bask in the warmth of the life-giving sun.*

It was a lunch meeting with her two fired friends that gave her a ray of hope again. Annie and Jerralyn had also been booted with only measly severance packages, and their own anger and betrayal rivaled Farron's. The three women got together for lunch and commiserated about their fears and doubts. They were all sickened by the terrible treatment they had received, especially since their bosses had kept their high-paying positions. It was all about profits and the bottom line, and now Farron, Annie, and Jerralyn were on the wrong side of that bottom line.

That's when Farron got the idea. Here were three very intelligent and skilled accountants out of work. Yet there were tons of smaller businesses that would need skills and talents like theirs, businesses that didn't need full-time accountants or perhaps needed someone to come in and train their own staff.

As the three women talked, the plan solidified, and they felt a sense of renewed excitement about their fuzzy futures. They would start their own business, help others, and never have to worry about bosses again. Now they would be their own bosses. They spent the rest of the day laughing and enjoying each other's company and the comfort of being among others experiencing the same challenge in life.

Farron silently thanked God for the great idea and, with her two new business partners, got busy planning their future.

Dear Lord, help me to see the positive that can come from the negative and the exciting opportunity present in each and every conflict. Share with me your heavenly wisdom and divine guidance, so that I may always stay clear and focused on the path you set out for me. Amen.

Are we weak and heavy laden, cumbered with a load of care? Precious savior, still our refuge; take it to the Lord in prayer.

Joseph M. Scriven

When your burdens become too great, God is always there to lead you beside still waters and restore your troubled soul.

At the first crack of daylight, it seems easiest,
O God, to simply pull the covers over my
head, turn over, and shut out the world. What
does this day hold? Can I get through it?
Don't I need the answers, reasons, and whys
taken care of before I venture forth? The task
feels overwhelming. Help me to see the
promise of a new day. Let me climb from bed
trusting the call of the future with the same
spirit as the bird who sings to greet the dawn,
even while it is still dark.

So don't be anxious about tomorrow. God
will take care of your tomorrow too. Live
one day at a time.

Matthew 6:34 TLB

BALANCE

Dani was an actress in Chicago and the mother of a two-year-old girl, Monica. Her husband had left abruptly just after Monica was born. These days, Dani wasn't quite sure whether she was an actor who mothered or a mother who acted. More than anything else, Dani wanted to be a good mother. But she also wanted to be a good actor, a good daughter, a good sister, and a good friend. Dani believed her chubby, dimpled redhead was too young to be in day care full-time. And yet she often had daytime auditions or needed quiet time to memorize lines. And then there was the little matter of making a living. Dani did temp work when she wasn't in a show and sometimes when she was, working as a receptionist or a restaurant hostess as her rehearsal schedule allowed.

One day, Dani was particularly conflicted. She had a small but pivotal role in a classic play, Anton Chekhov's *The Cherry Orchard*. Money was tight. She feared an overdraft at the bank once her rent check cleared because her child support from her former husband, which was supposed to be automatically deposited, hadn't come through. Thank goodness she had her downstairs neighbor, Mrs. Wilson, who counted it a privilege to hold Monica on her lap, take her to the neighborhood park, and make her favorite foods: box macaroni and cheese, green beans, and applesauce.

It is important to count your blessings while considering your misfortunes.

Dani trudged with a heavy heart to the subway stop that would take her to the theater downtown. Wouldn't it be better for Monica if she took a full-time job and put her in day care? That way, Monica could be on a predictable schedule, and Dani could finance lots of little extras, maybe even buy the two of them a small house by the time Monica was in kindergarten. Dani even considered moving back home to Iowa.

Her mother had offered to take care of Monica while Dani finished a degree in something "practical" like nursing or business. On this chilly, gray day, for which Dani hadn't put on enough layers, she wasn't sure of anything.

Dani did her best at the rehearsal, a second read-through. But she was distracted. At lunch break, an older actor, Gwendolyn, approached her and said, "Let's have lunch at that Greek place across the street. My treat."

Dani was surprised. She had barely exchanged two words with Gwendolyn. But she happily accepted. As they shared a huge plate of moussaka, Gwendolyn asked, "What's wrong, dear?"

Dani grimaced. "Does it show?"

"A little," Gwendolyn admitted. "At the first read-through, you made me cry. This time, all the intonations and pauses are right, but somehow the soul isn't there. You have a sad look in your eyes. I don't mean to be intrusive, but would it help to talk about it?"

Dani found herself pouring out her heart. Gwendolyn listened carefully, then said, "Well, dear, you can have it all but not all at once." She went on to tell how from a long life of passion, marriages, children, traveling, and theater, she had discovered that having it all was a myth. You couldn't have it all at the same time and keep your sanity. For the time being, she advised, Dani should concentrate on two things: her child and her acting. She would have time for everything else later.

When they went back to the rehearsal, Dani's voice throbbed with a quiet intensity. "What happened to you?" the director asked.

Dani and Gwendolyn merely looked at each other and smiled.

No matter how hard the winds of life blow, never let them knock the hope out of your sails.

Dear God, I pray to you today because I am not feeling very secure. My faith is shaky, and the ground beneath my feet feels as though it might cave in at any moment. Please be a strong and powerful presence in my life today, reminding me always that no matter what my life looks like, behind the illusion of chaos there is only the true perfection of your will. Amen.

Give to the winds thy fears;
Hope and be undismayed.
God hears thy sighs and counts thy tears,
God shall lift up thy head.

Look into the robin's nest, and see how the fledgling never doubts that it will be able to fly, trusting in the certainty of God's natural order designed for going on, becoming more, and finding wholeness.

Lord, the days ahead look pretty bleak, and my heart is filled with anxiety. Remind me that there is always a silver lining to every cloud and that each dark night gives way to the rising sun. Sometimes I get stuck in my self-pity. Help me to get unstuck, Lord, and to be strong and filled with hope. Amen.

THE CHRISTMAS ANGELS

It was December 23. My children and I lived in a very small house. I was a single mom, going to college and supporting my children alone. Christmas was looking bleak. I looked around me, realization dawning with a slow, twisting pain: We were poor.

Our tiny house only had two bedrooms. They were so small that my daughter's crib barely fit into one and my son's twin bed and dresser into the other. I made my bed every night on the living room floor.

It was late, almost 11, when my front door vibrated with a pounding fist. My heart thumping, I wondered who could be at my home so late. I peeked through the curtain on my front door to find several strangers grinning from ear to ear, their arms laden with boxes and bags.

Confused, but finding their joyous spirit contagious, I opened the door and grinned right back.

"Are you Susan?" A man stepped forward and slowly pushed a box at me.

Nodding stupidly, unable to find my voice, I was sure they thought I was mentally deficient.

"These are for you." A woman thrust another box at me with a huge, beaming smile. The porch light and the snow falling behind her cast a glow on her dark hair, lending her an angelic appearance.

I looked down into her box. It was filled with treats, a fat turkey, and all the makings of a Christmas dinner. My eyes filled with tears as the realization washed over me.

Finally coming to my senses, I invited them in. Following the man were two children, staggering with the weight of their gifts for my little family. This wonderful, beautiful family, total strangers to me, somehow knew exactly what we needed. They brought wrapped gifts, a full buffet to make on Christmas, and many "extras" that I could never afford. Visions of a beautiful, "normal" Christmas literally danced in my head. Somehow my secret hope for Christmas was materializing right in front of me. The desperate prayers of a single mom were heard, and I knew right then God had sent his angels my way.

My mysterious angels then handed me an envelope, gave me another round of grins, and hugged me. They wished me a merry Christmas and disappeared into the night as suddenly as they had appeared.

Amazed I looked around at the boxes strewn at my feet and felt the ache of depression suddenly being transformed into a childlike joy. I began to cry. I cried hard, sobbing tears of the deepest gratitude.

Remember, even after the darkest night, the sun shines, just as the rainbow follows the storm.

A great sense of peace filled me. The comfort of God's love reaching into my tiny corner of the world enveloped me. My heart was full. I fell to my knees amid all the boxes and offered a heartfelt prayer of thanks.

Suddenly I noticed an envelope amidst the boxes. Like a child, I ripped it open and gasped. A shower of money flitted to the floor. I began to count the bills, and my vision blurred with tears. I counted, then counted again to make sure I had it right. One hundred dollars.

There was no way my "angels" could have known it, but I had just received a disconnect notice from the gas company. I simply didn't have the money needed and feared we would be without heat by Christmas. The envelope of cash would guarantee us warmth. Suddenly we had all we needed and more.

I looked at my children sleeping soundly and I smiled the first happy, free-of-worry smile in a long, long time. My smile turned into a grin as I thought about tomorrow: Christmas Eve. One visit from complete strangers had magically turned a painful day into a special one we would always remember.

God, my challenges are many and my strengths few and far between. I can use your presence tonight to comfort me as I go through these trying times. Be my friend, my companion, my help in times of need. Keep me company tonight, until the coming of dawn brings me new hope for a better day. Amen.

Don't worry about anything; instead, pray about everything; tell God your needs and don't forget to thank him for the answers. If you do this you will experience God's peace, which is far more wonderful than the human mind can understand. His peace will keep your thoughts and your hearts quiet.

Philippians 4:6–7 TLB

TIME WELL SPENT

What comforts me?
What helps me to mend?
A call from my mom,
or a card from a friend.
A flower in bloom,
and the sound of soft rain.
A soft pair of socks,
a warm balm for my pain.
The sound of sweet laughter,
a sky clear and blue.
But nothing gives hope, God,
like time spent with you.

Faith is a gift we give ourselves.
Hope is a gift we give others.

Heavenly Hosts

When the cares of my heart are many, your consolations cheer my soul.

Psalm 94:19

STANDOFF

Being married to a police officer had its good and bad points. Sheri felt so protected when Brad was home, but when he was on the job, she couldn't help but feel anxious. Each day brought with it a new battle with her deepest fear: that Brad would not come home to dinner that night.

When Brad told her he had to take the night shift for three months, Sheri went weak in the knees. It was her worst fear of all. The night shift meant more crime, more danger, and more sleepless nights for her while she waited to hear Brad's key in the door.

His first month into the night shift was pretty benign. Most of his arrests were for thefts, vandalism, and loitering. But the night he didn't call in at his usual time, Sheri knew deep in her heart something had gone terribly wrong.

She called the police station, and the night-watch commander told her there was a standoff underway at a liquor store, with two police officers already down. He didn't have names yet.

Sheri set the phone nearby and turned on the TV. The late local news was reporting live across the street from the liquor store, and Sheri hoped they might show the officers involved. She watched in horror as the events unfolded, praying to God that Brad was off arresting some speeding teenager instead.

Two hours passed, and Sheri was in a panic. She couldn't take being alone, so she called her neighbor, Janey. Despite the late hour and two kids to deal with, Janey came right over and sat with Sheri, holding her hand as they watched the news. Luckily, Janey's mom was staying with them so she could watch the kids.

Janey's husband, a firefighter, had died two years earlier in the line of duty. She knew what Sheri was going through. What Sheri needed most was *not* to be told it would be all right, because

Giving comfort to someone else requires nothing more than listening as they talk and holding them as they cry.

sometimes it wasn't. Janey was living proof.

Janey knew that what Sheri needed was for her to just be there, to hold on to, to cry with, to pray with.

Another hour or so passed, and Sheri was exhausted. Janey continued to sit with her and hold her hand. Then the phone rang. Sheri stared at it, unable to move. Janey reached over and grabbed it, answering for Sheri. The look of relief on Janey's face said it all. Sheri took the phone. It was Brad's partner, Joe, calling to tell her that Brad had taken a shot to the arm in the standoff. Thankfully, he was okay and at the local hospital.

Sheri hung up, and without hesitation, Janey got her into her car and drove her to the hospital. When Sheri saw Brad, all she could do was smother him with kisses. She was just so grateful he was alive and even more grateful that he was going to finish his night shift on desk duty.

And she was truly, deeply grateful for Janey, who knew just what she needed to get her through the long, dark night. For the rest of their lives, Sheri would refer to Janey not as her neighbor or as her friend but as her personal, handpicked guardian angel.

Lord, my anxiety and fear are more than I can handle alone. Send me the gift of someone who knows my pain and understands my fears; someone who will not try to tell me to be strong and think positive, for I am not and I cannot. Send me a guardian who will stand with me as I face the darkness and walk with me to the light that waits on the other side. Amen.

Wherefore, comfort one another.

1 Thessalonians 4:18

A HAND TO HOLD

I don't need to be saved from hard times.
There are no wise words I should be told.
I don't need someone else to carry me,
I just need a hand to hold.
I know this will pass and I will smile
    again.
I know life won't always be this cold.
In the meantime could you sit with me a
    while?
I just need a hand to hold.
There will come a day when I am up
    on top,
Free and happy, fortunate and bold,
But today, the road's a little rocky here,
I just need a hand to hold.

INTERNET ANGELS

The doctors told us that my sister, Beth, would be gone by summer. She had been diagnosed with cancer. Reeling not only from the physical pain of her disease but also from the emotional pain of facing this challenge with a broken marriage and heart, my young sister bore loneliness and sorrow of the deepest magnitude.

I struggled to be a comfort to my sister while dealing with my own grief over her illness. I needed someone to talk to, a shoulder to cry on. I longed for someone who could understand what I was going through and who could help me be strong for my sister. I decided the Internet would be the perfect outlet for my grief, so I established a Web site devoted to inspirational stories. Over time, I met and shared stories with an amazing group of people. They had survived cancer; divorce; homelessness; the death of a child, a spouse, a parent, a sibling; disabling accidents; heartache; and pain of every kind. Somehow, life has a way of creating kindness and compassion in the wake of pain. I saw these wonderful qualities in my "online family."

I found writing about my sister's illness cathartic and shared many of our experiences online. Through my stories, Beth became a part of the lives of these gentle and loving people. Gifts and cards began to arrive for my sister. Relationships with people all over the world developed. As the cancer spread and my sister deteriorated, hundreds of letters and cards and, most of all, prayers poured forth. And through it all, as her life slowly seeped away, Beth's spirit began to transform. Simply being loved can create a miracle. It put Beth back onto a path of feeling loved.

For truly I tell you, whoever gives you a cup of water to drink because you bear the name of Christ will by no means lose the reward.

Mark 9:41

Eventually, I found an incredible Web site devoted to people undergoing chemotherapy. It opened up a world of kindness that became a rainbow during the last weeks of Beth's life. Daily cards, letters, and packages began arriving only two days after I signed Beth up for a Chemo Angel. She heard from not one but hundreds of angels who reached out with boundless empathy and heartfelt compassion. Between the dear friends Beth had made from my Web site family and the Chemo Angels, every single day of her life brought happy surprises of friendship. My sister's loneliness was beginning to ease away and was replaced with the thousands of strangers—angels—who unconditionally loved her and gave her back her smile.

Each day's mail brought stacks of envelopes and packages—all just for Beth. Her face, swollen, bruised, and scarred from the chemotherapy, surgeries, and many falls, was at last transformed with light and laughter, a gift from heaven wrapped in the love of strangers.

Each of these dear people created a haven from pain for my sister. Her bedroom was filled with constant reminders that God does send angels to do his work. These angels had a very short time to perform a miracle, but they accomplished it with the flurry of angel wings and the sparkle of heavenly dust. They showered love on my sister with such intensity and such zest that she could not help but allow her loneliness to evaporate in their warmth.

The week before she died, Beth and I made a pact. I would be a Chemo Angel and she would be a "Guardian Chemo Angel." She was delighted, her blue eyes lighting up as our pact was sealed with tears and a hug. It is a moment frozen forever in my heart.

She is gone now, and I am a Chemo Angel, as are many of my Web site members who touched Beth's life. We are keeping our pact together, and I have felt her with me many times as I have mailed off packages of love. This tradition of "angeling" has come full circle, and I have no doubt she is with me every step of the way.

God, today I pray to you, not for my own needs but for those who seek comfort from the storm. Today I ask you to provide them with a mighty fortress of love, mercy, and grace that they can rest under until the clouds of life pass overhead, revealing clear blue skies again. Amen.

When storms rage, keep sights fixed not down in despair but up toward the horizon, for that is where doves—friends, family, wise ones, pathfinders—will appear. They bring the message that a safe harbor is in sight.

Let me see your footsteps in those who
share the walk with me;

Help me feel your touch in the hands of
those who serve me;

Grant me hear your voice in those who
speak words of comfort and compassion;

Let me know your love through those who
do your work here on Earth.

*When you pass through the waters, I will be
with you; and through the rivers, they shall
not overwhelm you; when you walk through
fire you shall not be burned.*

Isaiah 43:2

IN GOD'S WORDS

As we go through our daily lives performing small acts of comfort and kindness, we never imagine the impact our actions might have. A hug, a pot of soup, a prayer, or even a short note—which may seem so inadequate in the face of a friend's loss—may make a greater impression on the recipient than we could ever dream.

Some time ago, my pen pal Muriel wrote to me about the death of her 24-year-old son in a car crash caused by a drunk driver. Muriel spilled her heart out to me. Her pain was obvious and stunning. What's more, she felt unfaithful to her Christian values because she couldn't bring herself to forgive the driver who caused the accident.

I quickly penned heartfelt words of condolence in a card and mailed it. Months went by without a reply. Then one spring day I received a letter from Muriel expressing her profuse gratitude. "Your words," she said, "were the words I clung to for comfort in the past months. You were the only one who understood. I carry your note in my wallet. It's nearly worn out."

I was ashamed to admit I couldn't even remember what I had said, except I do know that with God's help, I had shared the sincere feelings of a mother's heart.

It is a gift when we are given the opportunity to comfort another person.

A newspaper clipping fell from Muriel's letter. It told about the life and death of her precious son, about the trial of the drunk driver, and about the playground Muriel was donating to the town in her son's memory. It also contained the words of the note she cherished. It was the letter that brought her so much comfort—my letter. As I read the contents of my note, I found my words to be quite ordinary; yet they spoke directly to her need.

I'm still amazed that a few words enclosed in a sympathy card could have such a profound effect on the person receiving them. But the words were God's, not mine; and that's just what God is: Amazing!

Heavenly Father, you know the pain of losing a child. Visit my friend today and console her in her mourning. Touch her with your peace and comfort her with your love. Turn her sorrow into joy. Give her the courage to go on, warmed by the sunshine of your love and your caring presence. Amen.

Simple acts of love as small as grains of sand are doves of hope sent by your hand, vigilant God. Inspire us to keep searching for doves in a dark sky, for they remind us how many grains of sand make dune, shore, and desert, and we get your message and can keep traveling this journey.

HERE FOR YOU

I'll be here for you when life tosses you to
the ground,
When it seems like there's no one else
around.
I'll be here for you when you're
disappointed in yourself,
Or when you've been let down by someone
else.
I'll be here for you when what you loved is
gone,
And it's hard to even imagine you'll find
strength for moving on.
There's not a lot that I can really do,
but I'll be here for you.

What a wonderful God we have—he is the Father of our Lord Jesus Christ, the source of every mercy, and the one who so wonderfully comforts and strengthens us in our hardships and trials. And why does he do this? So that when others are troubled, needing our sympathy and encouragement, we can pass on to them this same help and comfort God has given us.

2 Corinthians 1:3–4 TLB

We have a friend in God. He loves us and watches over us and sends down his angels to guide us and keep us all the days and nights of our lives. We have a constant companion in God, who never leaves our side, who is with us forever in times of trouble and in times of joy.

MAYA'S SMILE

Maya was named after my favorite author and poet, Maya Angelou. And like her namesake, Maya is wise far beyond her six years. With her four front teeth missing and eyes that sparkle like the Fourth of July, she is a teeny, doll-like darling. Because she's had a lot of health problems, she is smaller than most girls her age, a fact that has made her self-conscious, but also more sensitive to others' feelings.

One day, when Maya was in kindergarten, she came home from school, bubbling over with excitement. "Mama, guess what!" she hurled at me as she bounced in the front door. "Guess what—there's a new girl in my class and she doesn't speak any English and I'm her new best friend. I decided today!" she proclaimed jubilantly.

"Honey, slow down." I told her, laughing. Maya does and says everything with exuberance. Finally, she slowed down enough to tell me about a new girl who arrived from Mexico that day. Her name was Stephanie, and that was the extent of her English. Her name.

So Maya took it upon herself to become Stephanie's best friend. It never occurred to her that the language barrier might be a problem. To children, communication is taken for granted. All Maya cared about was that this new little girl cried all day and had no one to talk to.

Open my eyes, O God, that I might notice the needs of others. Open my mouth; let me provide a comforting word when needed. Open my heart, that I may reach out in love to a hurting person.

At the class Halloween party, I met Stephanie. She clung to Maya like spaghetti noodles cooked together, scared and withdrawn from contact with anyone else. Never once smiling, she sat as the other kids played games, silently watching the laughter and the fun. The teacher later told me that Maya was the only one

Stephanie would sit with at lunch or play with at recess. She was afraid to speak and never participated in class.

The days flew by, and each day Maya would come home from school babbling about her day and what Stephanie had learned. I usually mumbled "that's nice, honey," too "busy" to take the time to really listen to my daughter. I never realized what I was missing until the day her teacher called and told me what a wonderful child Maya was, what a good friend, and so on. I was pleased, but the impact of what she was saying didn't sink in until I witnessed it firsthand when I went in to volunteer at the school.

The withdrawn, paralyzed-with-fear little Stephanie was now a radiant, happy child. Her big brown eyes were as sparkly as Maya's. And she smiled! I couldn't believe the transformation. As the teacher and I talked, I watched Maya and Stephanie together. Most of their communication was pointing, helping, gesturing. And smiling.

Maya would look into her little friend's eyes and smile the sweetest, widest smile that would melt your heart. Her teacher told me of the gradual change that had taken place. Day after day, Maya would sacrifice her free time to sit patiently with her scared little friend, often defending her to other kids, always kind, and never, ever giving up on Stephanie. My eyes filled with tears as she described my daughter's tremendous heart and selflessness.

When Maya and I were alone that night, I told her how proud I was of her and that she was a true friend. I asked her how she created this amazing friendship without a common language. My blue-eyed angel looked up at me and simply said, "I smiled."

Maya and Stephanie have been in the same class for several years now, their friendship cemented since kindergarten. Every time I see Stephanie, I remember the scared little girl and how my own little girl was a true friend. She is my hero.

God, let me be a rock today for someone else in need. Let me be the column that they can lean upon when their own strength fails them. Then will I have truly given back some of the wondrous blessings you have given me. Let me be a rock today, dear Lord. Amen.

God, give me the courage today to reach out to someone else in need. Give me the wisdom and discernment to help them overcome a challenge as you have always helped me. I have been given so much, now I want to give back. Help me to do this, God, and I will have fulfilled my greatest purpose for living. Amen.

THE BEST KIND

The best kind of comfort is the kind that
 comes
From tender loving care,
That only the people whom we love can
 give
In times of doubt and fear.
It matters not if they live far or close
Or what kind act they share,
For with friends who care to take the time,
We are blessed beyond compare.

*Time. We are given exactly 24 hours in each
day. How we account for it is our duty. How
we use it is our legacy.*

There is nothing weak about asking for the help we need to get us through the darkest times in our lives. That is why God made other humans, so that we may all be there for each other to offer love, hope, and comfort. We are angels to one another.

Great Spirit, I seek the peace only you can provide. Guide me through the darkest hours, and bring light into the shadows of my broken heart. You alone can heal me. You alone can give me the peace that passeth all understanding, Spirit. I open my heart to be filled with the light and the healing power of your comforting love, now and forever.

Forever Faithful

Even though I walk through the darkest valley, I fear no evil; for you are with me.

Psalm 23:4

IN A CHILD'S EYE

The adult was supposed to comfort the child. That's what Jackie always thought. But now as she sat on the couch huddling in fear, she wasn't so sure she knew how to provide her child with the security and comfort she once knew growing up.

The terrorist events of the last few days had made everyone in the country so afraid and suspicious. Jackie had not ventured anywhere, other than the local grocery store, for fear something else would happen.

Now the TV news was reporting a high alert for a possible attack, and Jackie felt frozen with fear. Her husband was at work, 20 miles away, and her five-year-old son, Toby, played in his room, oblivious to the turmoil and distress of the past few days. She wanted to grab him and hold him close for fear of losing him, but she knew her anxiety would only upset the boy.

If you sit down, you will not be afraid;

When you lie down, your sleep will be sweet.

Do not be afraid of sudden panic, or of the storm that strikes the wicked; for the Lord will be your confidence and will keep your foot from being caught.

Proverbs 3:24–26

Toby came into the room and saw Jackie sitting there, glued to the TV. She quickly changed the channel to a cartoon and forced a cheery smile. But Toby, like most children, knew when his mommy wasn't "right," and he sat next to her and held her hand.

"Mommy, don't be scared. God is watching us," he said, in his little boy voice, so full of innocence and purity.

Jackie didn't know how to respond, so she just squeezed his hand. Toby leaned against her for warmth, and they snuggled and watched cartoons together. Jackie tried to think positively, going over Toby's words in her head, but her paranoia and fear kept surfacing.

Again, Toby looked up at his mom and smiled. There was something in his eyes that made Jackie tremble. It was not fear but an incredible sense of *knowing* that she saw in her little boy's wide blue eyes. It was the look of someone completely at ease and confident with life. It was the look of faith.

Jackie felt her body relax, and her mind followed. She became absorbed in the silliness of the cartoon, and soon she was laughing out loud with Toby. As the day went on, Toby would look up at his mom often, with that same look of inner certainty that was far beyond his years.

And he would grab her hand and squeeze it, as if he knew she needed the constant reassurance.

The night came without incident, and Jackie let Toby sleep in his own bed for the first time since the attacks. She still didn't know what the future would hold, but she was beginning to believe that Toby was right. God was watching them, and all was right in their world, even if only for the night.

Heavenly Father, just knowing you are there brings me comfort and hope, even as the world seems so chaotic and cold outside my window. Just feeling your presence gives me courage and faith, even as those around me live in the shadow of fear and doubt. Just being with you, God, makes me stronger. I thank you for always being with me. Amen.

Keep me, today and every day,

Safe.

Sheltered.

Secure.

In the hollow of your hand.

Nothing provides comfort in times of trouble like wrapping yourself in a big, thick blanket of faith.

Lord, these days there are so many things to worry about and be afraid of. Help me to stay strong and focused so that I can take care of myself and provide encouragement and comfort to those who depend on me. Let me be the one they can turn to for hope and for help. Amen.

How comforting it is to know that when we lose control, God is there to take the reins.

Faith in a wise and trustworthy God, even in grievous times like these, teaches us a new math: subtracting old ways and adding new thoughts because sharing with God divides our troubles and sadness and multiplies unfathomable possibilities for renewed life.

Your faith has saved you; go in peace.

Luke 7:50

The Kiss of Life

It happened in slow motion and felt like a dream. We were four hours from home after a long road trip. The storm came sudden and furious, the snow so heavy I couldn't see the road. I immediately slowed down. I could feel in the pit of my stomach that this was dangerous. I was right.

I realized the road was nothing but thick ice. Suddenly, I felt the car sliding sideways. At 60 miles an hour, we jerked across the road, and the nightmare began.

I was helpless to control the car. The more I tried to keep the wheel straightened out, the more we just spun in circles across the freeway. I felt my body go numb and heard my nine-year-old daughter screaming, as if from far away.

One side of the car began to tilt, and as we started to flip, I thought *this is it, we're going to die*. Even my thoughts seemed to slow down in an unreal time warp. Nina's screams reverberated again and again, shattering the muffled silence of the world around us as we careened out of control.

Our car hit a pole in the median, spun sideways, began to flip again, and then—with a bone-crunching jolt—plopped back down hard and skidded sideways once more. Finally, as if a giant hand reached down from the heavens, we stopped.

Nina's screams softened to a whimper. I was shaking so hard I wondered if I was having a seizure. I turned to look at the kids, tears cascading down my cheeks. I began sobbing so hard I couldn't speak. My oldest son, Nick, was calm and reassuring. "It's over, Mom, it's over," he repeated, knowing I was in shock. The terror, which I had been too busy fighting for our lives to feel, was now very vivid.

We could have died. In the flash of an instant, our lives could have ended. I thought of my father, now on the other side, and wondered if he had watched, knowing we could be together again. God had other plans for me, and without a doubt, he spared our lives.

Grateful, so grateful, for them, I looked at our seat belts, snugly protecting us. I felt the bruises that were already developing from mine and knew they had saved us.

I called on your name, O Lord, from the depths of the pit; you heard my plea, "Do not close your ear to my cry for help, but give me relief!" You came near when I called on you; you said, "Do not fear!" You have taken up my cause, O Lord, you have redeemed my life.

Lamentations 3:55–58

Unbuckling, I crawled out of the car, in near-hysterics, to see the damage. The running board and side of the car were smashed and broken. The tires on the passenger side had been completely knocked off, and they lay rumpled and mangled. I realized later that this was another thing that saved us. The tires coming off stopped the car cold and kept us from flipping or spinning any farther.

Shivering from both the cold and the shock, I peered though the snow to see where we were. Three feet away was a deep gully. My heart did a flip-flop as I realized how close we had come to landing in that gully.

We eventually got help and got home, but I couldn't get over how close we had been to death. I still can't help wondering what it was God saved me for. He could very easily have called me back to him. The awful nightmare was a stark reminder that God is always there and is constantly aware of our needs. Every day I try to remember how protected we were and, with gratitude, hope that I can live up to his plans for me.

By this we know that we abide in him and he in us, because he has given us of his Spirit.

1 John 4:13 NASB

God of all comfort, I call to you in the darkness. Be my light. As the beacon that guides the distressed ship safely to shore, guide me now to the shores of your love, your strength, and your wisdom. For without you, I am blind and have no direction. Be my light. Be my comfort. Be my strength. Amen.

Unless the Lord had given me help, I would soon have dwelt in the silence of death. When I said, "My foot is slipping," your love, O Lord, supported me. When anxiety was great within me, your consolation brought joy to my soul.

LOOK WITHIN

The comfort we seek is always there
   through any challenge or test.
By looking inward we can glimpse the face
   of the one who cares best.

*You who have done great things, O God,
who is like you? You who have made me see
many troubles and calamities will revive
me again; from the depths of the earth you
will bring me up again. You will increase
my honor, and comfort me once again.*

Psalm 71:20–21

The joy of the Lord is your strength.

Nehemiah 8:10 NASB

Sing, pray, and keep God's ways unswerving; so do thine own part faithfully, and trust God's word; though undeserving, thou shalt yet find it true for thee. God never forsook at need the soul that trusted God indeed.

George Neumark

In time of affliction we commonly meet with the sweetest experiences of the love of God.

John Bunyan

But we are not of those who shrink back and are destroyed, but of those who have faith and keep their souls.

Hebrews 10:39

ENOUGH TO MOVE A MOUNTAIN

It was 30 minutes past the time my five-year-old son was supposed to be home. I called the home of our neighbors, where Nicholas had been playing. No answer. I hung up, paced the kitchen, and called again. The phone rang 20 times, still no answer. Slipping into my sandals, I walked three houses down the street and knocked on the door. No answer. My heart sank as I peeked around the driveway and saw that it was empty. Panic began to grip my entire body like a vice. Heart pounding, I ran back to our home and began to search the house. Perhaps Nicholas had come in and was hiding. He loved to play tricks. I began shouting to him that Mommy was scared and to please come out. The stillness of the house made my palms sweat.

My search revealed nothing but an empty house, my voice echoing his name. I began a panic-stricken prayer for help. My heart racing, my hands shaking, I begged the Lord to protect my son, wherever he was. At once I felt peace and comfort. My son would be safe.

Again I searched our home and yard thoroughly. I walked up and down the street, knocking on the doors of any of the neighbors who might have seen him. No Nicholas. Numb with disbelief, I phoned my husband, the neighbors, anyone I could think of who could help look for Nicholas. Then, knowing I had no other choice, I called the police. I heard my own voice report my son missing. My faith faltered. I felt as if I was hearing someone else's words.

My legs like rubber, I went again to the neighbors' house. I rang the doorbell, pounded on the door, and yelled for my child as loud and long as I could stand it. Hysterical at this point, I stumbled back home and found a photo of my son for the police. I couldn't believe I was actually doing this. Sobbing, I remembered the verse about faith being able to move mountains. Closing my eyes, I again prayed for God to give me my child back.

Immediately I again felt a certainty that Nicholas was okay. I didn't hear but felt the words: *Have faith.* A peace came over me. I stopped doubting.

The police arrived; my family and friends arrived, and the neighborhood was teeming with people calling Nicholas's name. I felt compelled to try one more time at the neighbors' house. Banging on the door, I nearly fell inside when it suddenly opened and three little faces peered out at me.

> *Find rest, O my soul, in God alone; my hope comes from him. He alone is my rock and my salvation; he is my fortress. I will not be shaken.*
>
> Psalm 62:5–6

One of them belonged to my son.

"Nicholas!" The door almost shut again. I'm sure the children were frightened by the shrieking woman on the porch. I reached in and yanked my child out. We stood on the porch, and I could only sob and hold my son. When things settled down and I was able to speak again, I asked Nicholas why no one answered the phone or the door.

"Adam and Libby's mom went to the store. She told us not to go to the door or answer the phone," was his honest child logic. "Aw, Mom . . . I was okay." I couldn't help laughing. The longest two hours of my life, and all because children were being obedient. Yet through it, I had God's comforting assurance that all would be well, and in the end, my son was safe and home again. My faith grew tenfold that afternoon. I learned to trust in God's comfort and never doubt him again.

God, bring me comfort, for today I am fearful. Bring me faith, for today I am doubting. Bring me love, for today I feel alone. Most of all, bring me hope, for today I am uncertain about my future. Amen.

What God Will Do for Us

When our strength fails us, God's suc-
ceeds.

When our light dims, God glows.

When our faith stumbles, God stands
straight.

When our mind doubts, God knows.

*This is my comfort in my distress, that your
promise gives me life.*

Psalm 119:50

*God is our refuge and strength, a very pres-
ent help in trouble.*

Psalm 46:1

When darkness falls upon me,
Your comfort, Lord, I cherish;
My confidence is in my God,
You'll never let me perish.

Christ holds out his hands to us and bids us come to him for rest. No burden is too great or sorrow too deep that he cannot ease it with his touch.

Faith is like a good friend that is always with us, assuring us that everything will be all right, even when it's going all wrong.

By his strength,
Weakness is made strong.
By his generosity,
My life is full and blessed.
By his grace,
Sin is vanquished.
By his sacrifice,
I may be saved.

We forget things so often, whether it's our car keys, our appointments, or what we were looking for in the next room. It's hard to remember everything in these overwhelming times. Yet God never forgets those who he holds in the palm of his hand.

Prayers for Peace

Peace I leave with you; my peace I give to you. I do not give to you as the world gives. Do not let your hearts be troubled, and do not let them be afraid.

John 14:27

COMFORT SOUP

Whenever Gina felt frightened, alone, or depressed, she could always count on her mom to come over with a big pot of hot chicken noodle soup. Gina referred to it as Comfort Soup and told her mom over and over again that she could make a killing if she ever bottled and marketed her soothing concoction.

But the day Gina's mom died, there was nothing that would comfort her. Not the love of her friends or her puppy, Charlie, or all the soup in the world.

For weeks, Gina mourned her mom, Sara, who had passed away after a long battle with breast cancer. Although Sara had been winning and losing to cancer for years, she had been cancer-free the last two years, and Gina had gotten used to thinking of her mom as healthy and vibrant.

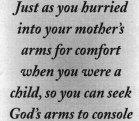

Just as you hurried into your mother's arms for comfort when you were a child, so you can seek God's arms to console you now that you're grown.

When the cancer returned this time, it returned with a vengeance.

Now Gina was left to carry on without the woman she adored, her best friend, her mom. Her good friends did their best to help Gina through the grieving, but often Gina just wanted to be alone, especially on the really tough days when the hopeless-ness and despair felt so heavy, she thought she would suffocate.

She was having one of those days when something compelled her to clean out her junk drawers. She had been sitting around crying for days, and now she had the strange urge to get up and do something, anything, to get her mind focused. So she attacked her two kitchen junk drawers with a fury she had never before experi-enced when it came to cleaning.

In the process of cleaning the second drawer, Gina found a sealed envelope. She couldn't remember putting it there, and she opened it with some uncertainty. Upon seeing the pink parchment paper inside, Gina began weeping.

Her mom always wrote on pink parch-ment paper. It was her favorite, and Gina recognized it instantly. She held it to her lips for a long minute before reading it. There, in her mom's distinct and dainty penmanship, was the recipe for her mom's famous Comfort Soup.

Gina read the recipe over and over again, weeping softly. Then, she smiled for the first time since her mom had died. She put the recipe on the counter, abandoned the junk drawer cleanup program, and set about gathering the ingredients to make the Comfort Soup.

Luckily, she had everything she needed, including some leftover chicken, and before long a pot was simmering on the stove. Gina breathed deeply, taking in the fragrance of the soup. The memory of her mom was so intense, she thought she might turn around and find her standing there, telling her to add more salt or drop in a bay leaf or two.

When the soup was ready, Gina took out a big bowl and poured herself a heaping serving. She sat down alone at the kitchen table and began to eat, savoring every bite as if it were her first. And when she was finished, she treated herself to a second bowl before cleaning up and putting the leftovers away.

Then she called two of her friends and asked if they would like to see a movie. It would be her first time out into the world since her mom died, but something had shifted for Gina. She felt comforted, knowing that she would always have her mom around. It was time to go forward with her own life again.

After all, her mom would have wanted it that way.

Thank you, God, for the little things that bring us joy. Thank you for the gifts of friends and family and for the small pleasures of daily life. Thank you for the minor miracles that occur each day, when we have open hearts and open eyes to see with. Thank you, God, for small comforts that fill our hearts with peace.

At the end of each difficult walk with grief as our companion, there's a place where the spirit can rest and find peace.

Dear God, your love embraces me like the warmth of the sun, and I am filled with light. Your hope enfolds me in arms so strong, I lack for nothing. Your grace fills me with the strength I need to move through this day and all its tribulations. Your presence forever reminds me that my beloved friend is always with me, no matter how much time passes. For these gifts you give me, eternal love, eternal peace, and most of all, eternal friendship, I thank you, God.

COMFORT

Comfort means different things to different people . . . a warm conversation, a bowl of mashed potatoes, a familiar face. We all need comfort. Life disappoints. We all need to know where to run when it gets to be too much. We all need to know how to tend to ourselves when we need comfort from the storms of life.

It's too easy sometimes to just keep going, to push ahead, to work through, to ignore the pain, to take a pill and sleep until morning. But sometimes what we need is a good cry, a short pity party, a call for help. It's the human condition. We've all been there. Yet, there's some myth of strength that whispers in our ears, "Big boys and girls don't cry."

Actually nothing could be further from the truth. What we need is to know when to cry and have the courage to do so. Only then can we move ahead with life.

ASK AN ANGEL

Blessed Angel up above,
Comfort me in arms of love.
Supreme Being in the sky,
Give my body strength to try.
Gentle Giant watching me,
Let your courage set me free.
Blessed Angel up on high,
Give my spirit wings to fly.

Loving God, comfort us when the world is too much for us, when we can't seem to find our way, when success eludes us and friends desert us. Comfort us when we are afraid, when we feel alone, and most of all, as we face death. We need you, God. We need the comfort only you can give.

Visiting beside still, tranquil waters,
I find peace. Like a shell, I carry it
home to hold against my ear and be
soothed again and again by its repeated
message.

I feel your presence, Faithful Lord, and accept
your gift to me of a new day, which arrives as
surely as dawn follows night. In that assur-
ance, I can move ahead, one day at a time,
knowing that no matter what came before,
each page turns to a promised new one.

Let the peace of heart that comes from
Christ be always present in your hearts and
minds.

Colossians 3:15 TLB

PHOTOGRAPHIC EVIDENCE

They had always been best friends. Still, when twin sisters Joan and Joanne fought, the grudge match often lasted for months. This time, it had lasted two years.

The battle began over a disagreement about their elderly mother, who needed round-the-clock care for Alzheimer's. Joan had wanted their mom to move into her large four-bedroom home. Joanne thought their mom would be better off in a facility with 24-hour nurses available and doctors on call. The argument had turned into a rift, then into a full-scale war that went on much longer than it should have, because both women were stubborn and each refused to give in to the other.

On the day their mother died, the war between them hung over their heads like a thick, black cloud. As they came together to plan the funeral, they still refused to reconcile, even though they were both grieving inside. Each put on a proud and controlled front as they argued over where to bury their mom and what kind of funeral to have.

Their husbands and children stayed out of their way, knowing better than to try to referee a boxing match that was out of control. Throughout the funeral and burial, Joan and Joanne did not even look at each other. The tension between them was so thick even the minister giving the ceremony looked concerned.

In times of hopelessness and despair, we can turn to those we love most for comfort. They know us better, love us stronger, and inspire us more. They care for us when we cannot care for ourselves.

When the funeral ended, everyone converged at Joan's for a quiet meal. There, she was like the queen of her castle, bustling about and taking care of everyone as Joanne sat in the corner with her family. But at one point, Joan disappeared, and Joanne felt a sudden urgency to go find her sister.

She found Joan in a back bedroom, curled on the floor like a child, weeping softly. Joanne swallowed hard and held her sister, rocking her twin in her arms as she, too, began to weep. For almost 20 minutes, the two sisters cried and mourned. When they finally stopped, Joanne looked up and smiled.

Hanging on the wall above them was a photo of the two of them as young girls, standing side by side with huge smiles on their faces. They looked like the two happiest people in the universe; happy to be alive, happy to be together.

Joan looked up, too, and the photo made her smile as well. They sat there for another few minutes, just letting all of the emotions roll over and through them. Then, they got up and went back into the living room hand in hand. Never again did they speak of the problems that had led to their time apart. They had lost their mom, but they still had each other, and nothing would ever come between that love again.

*Lord, comfort me when my heart is breaking,
give me peace when I feel that all is lost.
Rebuild my shattered faith when I no longer
believe in miracles. Help me to see that I am
already blessed with all that I need to be
happy. Amen.*

When my heart cries out
To heaven above
God demonstrates
The measure of his love.
He showers me
With grace and peace
From sorrow's hold he gives release.

See the home of God among mortals. He will dwell with them as their God; they will be his peoples; and God himself will be with them, he will wipe every tear from their eyes.

Revelations 21:3

God's blessings
are greater than the sum
of our burdens.
They calm our spirits
through the darkest night,
the deepest sorrow,
the sweeping winds
of change.
God's blessings bring the light,
the joy, the peace,
which surpasses
all understanding.

A Slice of Comfort

Just before Thanksgiving, Jack was diagnosed with a terminal disease. He was given six months to live, and he moved in with his son's family to live out the rest of his days.

Family and friends wondered what they could say to Jack to express their regret and sorrow over his illness. They knew Jack didn't want to be showered with pity, but they didn't know how to reach out to him and show they cared.

Julie, a family friend, decided to express her care and concern by baking Jack an apple pie to help him celebrate Thanksgiving. The pie was a long time in the making. Twice, she had to throw away a batch of dough and start over. But when she saw the pleasure that pie gave Jack, she knew God had put the idea in her heart.

At Christmas, Jack requested "another one of those good apple pies." He feasted on it for a whole week. Valentine's Day provided another excuse to bake, and so did the Easter holiday. By this time the disease had spread, and as she made her pie, Julie prayed that Jack would live out his short life in comfort and peace.

On Mother's Day, the family gathered again, but Jack was getting weaker and losing his appetite. Still, Julie baked another pie and prayed for him.

When Father's Day came, Jack's son told Julie to hold off on baking until he felt better. She told Jack she had the bag of apples ready and would

Sharing our experience, strength, and hope is a wonderful way to let someone else know we care about them and understand their suffering.

make another pie as soon as he was feeling better. Soon Jack sent word that he was ready for his apple pie. Suspecting that this would be his last, Julie put extra prayers and extra effort into the baking.

By this time, Jack was very weak. He wasn't eating much, but his eyes sparkled when he saw the pie. Over the next two weeks, the apple pie went down one sliver at a time. It was the only food Jack could handle.

By Independence Day, Jack was gone, but just before his death, he spoke repeatedly about those apple pies, baked with love and prayers during his months of illness.

Julie didn't trust herself to say the right things to Jack, so she let her actions speak for her. A simple pie was used by God to bring peace and joy to a dying man.

Thank you, Father, for the privilege of serving you in your ministry of comfort. Show me the small ways I can help to ease the pain and sorrow of those who suffer. Help me to bring your message of hope and peace to those who have lost heart, so they won't be afraid. Amen.

TAKE THIS CUP

Take this cup of comfort,
Drink fully of God's love,
Taste the care with which it's made,
By angels from above.
Absorb the healing essence,
Of its warm and tender glow,
And quench your spirit's deepest thirst
With love's unceasing flow.

I will turn their mourning into joy, I will comfort them, and give them gladness for their sorrow.

Jeremiah 31:13b

God, be with my friend. Be the unseen arm around his shoulder. Carry his pain. Give him peace. Focus his mind on what matters most. Give him some sense of purpose today that is outside of the difficulties he is facing. Give him laughter and hope. Remind him that life is bigger than any one season. Only you, God, can be with my friend in every situation. Whisper to him that he is loved. Don't let him forget. Amen.

It takes very little sun shining through a storm to create a rainbow, very little light through a prism. God uses our tears as the showers.

REACHING OUT

The wind and rain had not let up for two days, and Lisa was beginning to panic. Her husband, Ray, was out of town on business, and she was home alone with two small boys and the possibility of a hurricane moving into her region by nightfall.

She'd had the good sense to go out and get food and supplies before the rains became too heavy, so she felt some small sense of security. Still, the weather was getting nastier by the second, and she was concerned about flooding in their basement and living room.

She heard a loud crashing sound outside her bedroom window and peeked through the blinding rain to see her elderly neighbor struggling to get her trash cans into the garage. Lisa quickly gathered up the boys, and they ran outside to help their neighbor.

Mrs. Rios was in her late 80s and lived with her daughter, who had just been hospitalized with pneumonia. Lisa knew that Mrs. Rios had a part-time nurse who often came to help her, but with the horrible weather, the nurse could not get into their area. She and the boys did what they could to help Mrs. Rios get inside and get settled just as a hurricane warning blared over the radio and TV.

The noise of the world is deafening, but God's peace is resounding.

It seemed like only seconds passed as the wind speed tripled, and Lisa and her boys realized if they didn't get back to their own home, they might not be able to get to their basement in time. Lisa saw the look of terror in Mrs. Rios's eyes and realized the old woman did not have a basement. She could not leave the old woman alone. It would take all of her strength to get Mrs. Rios back to their house and into their basement.

The boys helped as best they could, but they were so small. Lisa had to almost carry Mrs. Rios across the lawn, into her home, and help her carefully down into the basement. Luckily, it was still dry and the sandbags at the ground-level windows had held back any leaks.

The four of them huddled together, listening to a battery-operated radio for word of the storm damage. They could hear the wind rage outside and the rain turn to hail, bashing against the house at an angle. Lisa cringed as a window upstairs broke, and she held the boys close.

As the noise of the storm increased, Mrs. Rios began to sing. Through the wind and hail, the old woman sang a song in Spanish, a soothing lullaby. Lisa was amazed at how the woman's delicate voice cut through the noisy storm. The lilting song comforted her and instantly calmed the boys.

Within a few minutes, the boys were asleep. Lisa closed her eyes and listened as Mrs. Rios sang away the storm. As the wind died down and the hail turned into a moderate rain, Lisa realized the worst had passed them. According to the radio, the eye of the hurricane was no longer over their area.

They were safe. As Lisa looked at her boys, sleeping peacefully, she was thankful for reaching out to help Mrs. Rios, who, in turn, helped them.

God, I know that you often work your wondrous miracles in the form of other humans. Thank you for the blessings of peace received from friends, family, and even strangers who come into our lives like angels sent from above. Amen.

Knowing I am heard, sought, and found gives me peace enough to hold on.

A PRAYER FOR COMFORT

Shelter me, God, from this cold, windy
    storm
That threatens to topple my boat.
Comfort me, Lord, as I draw in my sails,
And help me to stay afloat.

*We need your comfort, God. We need to feel
your hand. We need a reminder that we are
not alone in this world. We don't always
listen, that's true. Yet, we need to hear you
speak to us. We busy ourselves with the accom-
plishments of life, doing this and doing that.
But when it comes right down to it, we know
that life itself comes from you. Help us to live
this life with its challenges and fears. Teach us
to walk through our days with confidence. It's
not that we can face anything, but that with
you we never face anything alone. Amen.*

The Lord is my shepherd, I shall not want. He makes me lie down in green pastures; he leads me beside still waters; he restores my soul.

Psalm 23:1–3

God invites us to the one place we can go to find comfort and peace: his loving arms.

The sheep run to the shepherd for comfort. In the safety of his arms, they feel at peace.

Freedom from Fear

Do not fear, for I am with you, do not be afraid, for I am your God; I will strengthen you, I will help you, I will uphold you with my victorious right hand.

Isaiah 41:10

SEPTEMBER 12, 2001

I watched this morning as my three-year-old built a tower with his blocks, then made his hand into an airplane and crashed it into the tower. The tower collapsed. Sickened, I gathered the blocks and put them away.

Last night, I awoke to the sound of jets flying overhead. I quietly opened the doors and slipped out into the garden in my nightgown, my heart pounding. My arms wrapped around my shaking body, I looked up into the starry night sky and saw the jets from nearby Hill Air Force Base flying overhead. I slid back into bed with my children, who had been having nightmares. It was a long night.

> *But you, O Lord, are a shield around me, my glory, and the one who lifts my head.*
>
> Psalm 3:3

When I went to fill my gas tank last night, I found others in my community in a quiet state of shock. A television was tuned to the news, and people soberly watched the events unfold, minute by horrifying minute.

Today I let my exhausted children sleep in and then gave them the day off from school. We headed out of town for a day of fun, horseback riding, and a visit to the candy factory. My heart was heavy, my spirit numb.

And then freedom rang.

Driving the 45 minutes to the animal park, I was amazed to discover just how much pride my fellow citizens have. Neighborhood after neighborhood was lined with flags. Local Boy Scout troops had been out until very late and up very early in the morning donating thousands of American flags to the homes in Utah.

When I got on the freeway, I saw something I had never seen before. Each overpass had an American flag attached to the outside, so every passing car would drive beneath our beloved Stars and Stripes.

And then I began to notice the marquees of car dealerships, malls, business centers. "God Bless America," over and over, lit up brilliantly alongside the freeway. Gone were the proclamations of sales and discounts. In their place was love for a country that no force is strong enough to destroy. "Freedom Will Prevail" announced one sign. *Darn right,* I thought.

I learned that the Air Force jets that I had heard all night were actually patrolling our skies and keeping watch over Utah. They were guarding us while we slept.

Prayer vigils all over the country. Long lines at the blood banks. Our president praying and quoting scripture. Radio stations playing songs of dedication to the victims and rescuers. Ordinary citizens reaching out. My nine-year-old daughter praying for peace and safety for the people who were hurt. Our congress members singing "God Bless America" in the sweetest, most off-key, most moving rendition I have ever heard. I cried. God has shed his grace upon us, despite the horror that crashed into us yesterday.

The good HAS prevailed. Our country stands stronger, firmer, and closer to God. Our faith is deepened, and kindness from all over the world floods our country's borders and its citizens' souls. And today, my heart filled with gratitude and pride to be an American citizen. We will forever be the land of the free and the home of the brave.

Lord, in the difficult and frightening days ahead, we need you more than ever to provide us with the comfort of a higher power to guide us and keep us from harm. We ask you to be the mighty shield that stands between us and harm's way. We pray to you to walk beside us in the darkness as we face the challenges of the unknown. Amen.

I will not leave you orphaned; I am coming to you. In a little while the world will no longer see me, but you will see me; because I live, you also will live.

John 14:18–19

SOMETHING TO HOLD ONTO

God, give me something real fuzzy and
　warm
To hold onto when sunny skies threaten to
　storm.
Give me a doll to hang onto real tight,
When I'm lost in the darkness with no
　hope in sight.
Give me a blankie to wrap myself in
When the world gets too cold and my
　head starts to spin.
For even though I am full grown and
　mature,
I could still use some help to feel safe and
　secure!

I sought the Lord and he answered me, and delivered me from all my fears.

Psalm 34:4

I need you Lord,
To cast out fears,
To soothe my heart,
To dry my tears.

The heart that trembles in fear needs nothing more than to know it is not alone.

No matter how charmed our lives,

no matter how successful we are,

no matter that others look at us with envy,

no matter that most of the time we feel
strong,

no matter that we know how good we
have it,

each of us has moments

of fear,

of anxiety,

of feeling overwhelmed,

of worry for our future.

At those troubled times

God steps in,

soothes our souls,

gives us comfort,

holds us in the embrace

of loving arms.

BLUE JEAN ANGELS

Tammy gathered up her children, all 25 of them, and gave them their bus seat assignments. The class was going on a field trip into the city for the grand opening of the natural history museum. Tammy loved these field trips, and this time she was thrilled to have five parent chaperones to help her.

As the kids boarded the bus, Tammy felt a strange sensation in her stomach. She brushed it off as excitement mixed with a bit of anxiety and got on the bus.

The trip took them through some gorgeous New England backcountry, and the trees and leaves displayed the bold colors of autumn. Tammy soaked up the beauty, wishing they could get out for a while and enjoy the scenery. She got her wish—but not in the way she had hoped.

The popping sound took everyone by surprise, and no one had time to react before the bus tilted and careened into a ditch. A tire had burst into pieces, and the driver had lost control. Now the bus and its occupants lay sideways.

Tammy had fallen onto three children, and she could hear screams and moans all around her. She struggled to get some sense of footing so she could assess the extent of the damage. When she looked around her, she saw that three of the adults were unconscious. The other adults appeared to be wounded, but she could not tell how serious their injuries were.

Somehow, she made it through the window of the bus and crawled out, surveying the scene and looking for any cars along the rural back road. Realizing she was alone, she lowered herself back into the bus and faced the situation with a mixture of fear and determination. She was the teacher. She was in charge.

There were so many injured children, and Tammy quickly became panicky, the tears filling her eyes as she struggled to find the emergency aid kits under the bus seats.

She was beginning to think maybe she couldn't handle the situation, and her panic grew to total horror as she noticed blood on some of the seats. She stopped, frozen with fear, and prayed to God for someone to help her.

But she was the only adult able to function. She was alone.

As she scrambled to help who she could, she heard a voice yelling from outside the bus. Then another voice and another. Tammy maneuvered herself toward the window and crawled up. She came face to face with five young men in jeans and

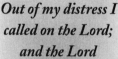

Out of my distress I called on the Lord; and the Lord answered me and set me in a broad place. With the Lord on my side, I do not fear.

Psalm 117:5–6

T-shirts, crawling onto the upside of the bus. They grabbed Tammy and pulled her out, then three of them went inside the bus and pulled out the other children and adults one by one. Another of the young men called 911 on his cell phone. Then they sat with Tammy and the other conscious children and parents and waited for the ambulances.

Tammy learned that the young men were members of a rock band traveling to their next gig in the city. They went to their car and pulled out snacks and sodas for the terrified children and even sang a song a cappella to try and take the kids' minds off their injuries. As the sirens approached, Tammy's heart lifted, and she felt a wave of relief wash over her.

The paramedics reported that no one had been seriously hurt, and Tammy thanked God and the five young men with all her heart. She had never been alone. God had sent angels in blue jeans just when she needed them.

Lord, I know your ways are mysterious, and your messengers often come in the least likely of forms. Help me to always recognize the amazing and abundant blessings in my life, even if they turn out to be much different than what I had wanted or expected. Amen.

Lord, grant me the strength to stand
   unassisted,
And the courage to walk on my own.
But not yet.
Please walk with me
Until I am ready to go alone.

I will not leave you comfortless;
I will come to you.

John 14:18 KJV

Do not be afraid, little flock, for it is your Father's good pleasure to give you the Kingdom.

Luke 12:32

God's love is a garden where we are nurtured, protected, and made strong, so weeds of sorrow and fear cannot choke us out.

Lord, let me walk in your shadow awhile, so that no evil comes near me. Let me stand beneath your protective umbrella, so that the blinding rains do not affect me. Let me hide in your glorious light until my strength and courage return. Amen.

What have I to dread, what have I to fear, leaning on the everlasting arms?

Elisha A. Hoffman

Therefore I tell you, do not worry about your life, what you will eat or what you will drink, or about your body, what you will wear. Is not life more than food, and the body more than clothing? Look at the birds of the air; they neither sow nor reap nor gather into barns, and yet your heavenly Father feeds them. Are you not of more value than they? And can any of you by worrying add a single hour to your span of life? And why do you worry about clothing? Consider the lilies of the field, how they grow; they neither toil nor spin, yet I tell you, even Solomon in all his glory was not clothed like one of these.

Matthew 6:25–29

MOON PIES

Jean watched dreams fall apart all around her as the tornado ripped through her cul-de-sac. From her safe position on a hill about a mile away, she could see the roofs and walls of neighbors' homes being torn from their foundations like pieces of cheap cardboard.

Her own home was pretty much flattened when she finally made it down to her street that afternoon. Once the storms cleared, she had reluctantly left her perch on the hill. The street looked like a war zone. Doors and walls from one house sat on top of the doors and walls of houses two blocks away. Jean's car was gone, probably in the next town somewhere.

She stood surveying the disaster scene with a sense of numbness. She was in shock, she knew; yet she couldn't really feel anything. Not sadness, not despair. Not even anger. Just plain numbness.

Mechanically, she moved through the rubble of her home and looked for anything she could use. There were clothes she knew belonged to her neighbors and a refrigerator that she didn't recognize as her own. The cleanup would take many painstaking days. Right now, all Jean wanted was to find something that was once hers. Anything. She didn't care what.

Take heart, it is I; do not be afraid.

Mark 6:50

Even one shoe would have filled her heart with hope.

What she did find made her laugh out loud. Sitting atop somebody else's luggage was a box of Moon Pies. They were Jean's favorite snack, and she seriously doubted they belonged to anyone else. She remembered she had stocked up before the storms hit, knowing she would need her special comfort food more than anything. She hadn't yet had the chance to eat any when the first wave of rain and winds hit. By the time she knew what was happening, the tornado watch had turned into a warning, and she was off in the opposite direction of the oncoming funnel cloud.

Now she held the box of Moon Pies in her hand, and for the first time she felt something stir within. She began to weep softly, then the tears came harder, and she sobbed deep and hard and without any concern for who might see or hear her. As she cried, she noticed another box sitting just a few feet away. She crawled over to it and picked it up, her tears staining the cheerful image on the box of happy Moon Pie faces.

When she felt as though she had no more tears to cry, she took the boxes of Moon Pies and went in search of the nearest Red Cross shelter, where she would bunk for the night and seek what assistance she could get to rebuild her home and her life.

And she would share her Moon Pies with anyone who wanted one, knowing that sometimes the smallest things bring comfort in times of distress.

Lord, your love is the foundation we build our lives upon. Your grace is the structure we surround ourselves with, a stronghold in our day of trouble. Your comfort is the roof that shelters us from the mighty winds that threaten to destroy us. In your house, Lord, we find an endless supply of courage, conviction, and faith. Amen.

MY GUIDE

When the path before my eyes
is strewn with rock and debris,
my crippling doubts begin to rise
and I fear what will happen to me.
That is when I look within
for the strength and comfort I need,
to assure me that when things get rough
my God will take the lead.

The moment you learn to look within for the comfort and strength you need is the moment when nothing outside you can ever again shake the foundation of your faith.

Have courage for the great sorrows of life and patience for the small ones; and when you have laboriously accomplished your task, go to sleep. God is awake.

Victor Hugo

No matter what may be the test,

God will take care of you;

Lean, weary one, upon his breast,

God will take care of you.

Civilla D. Martin

After the Rain

*Blessed are the poor in spirit, for
theirs is the kingdom of heaven.
Blessed are those who mourn, for
they will be comforted.*

Matthew 5:3–4

VOICE MAIL FROM HEAVEN

She was 28, and my vibrant, feisty,
beautiful sister was gradually becoming a
vague shell of herself, replaced with the
side effects of her brain tumor and med-
ications.

Knowing I was losing my sister broke
my heart, but watching her suffer shattered my soul. Her body began to shut
down; what was left of her abilities faded
one by one. She was paralyzed on her right

side, and her face and body became tremendously swollen from the steroids that controlled the swelling in her brain. She became weaker and weaker.

However, the most painful loss for her was the ability to communicate. Her speech, at first affected by only a slight slur that sounded more like an accent, increasingly dropped off into broken sentences. The words were increasingly unable to make their way to her lips. Only an occasional word escaped here and there.

Earth has no sorrow that Heaven cannot heal.

Thomas Moore

Angel was devastated at not being able to form the words that her heart felt and needed to say. Always a "talker," as are all the women in our family, I knew how hard this was for her. I often saw tears trickle down her cheeks with the frustration of not being able to bring the words to the surface. I too missed her ability to talk. I longed for our giggling sister-talks. I missed the hours of babble and laughter that sisters share. I missed the sound of her voice and her contagious, delightful laughter.

The morning after she left this life for the next, I awoke with the deepest aching pain I've ever known. I would have given anything for just one more moment, one more hug, one more "love ya" from my sister. I was happy for her that she was with God now, free of pain and full of joy again, but I missed my sister. And then I picked up the phone to call Mom.

Hearing the stutter tone that told me I had voice mail, I dialed in to retrieve the messages. The computer-generated voice informed me that I'd had a message saved for 100 days. I listened for the message, ready to delete whatever I once felt necessary to save. Nothing seemed important to me anymore.

"Hi Sooz, it's me." Angel's voice.

I choked with the sobs that immediately came as I heard her voice, full of life and love once again, her words clear and steady. She began to babble about everything and nothing, just like she always did. I found myself laughing for the first time in ages, as the sound of her "I forgot my point" message played on. Again I played it. And again. Over and over until I felt sunshine in my soul. "Love ya!" she said, and I saved the message for another 100 days, wondering when I would hear it again. I then realized I had saved dozens of her messages, not knowing that one day they would be so precious. I smiled at the thought.

Tears of gratitude slipped down my face. The absolute comfort I felt in this glorious gift was inexplicable. It wrapped around me like a warm quilt, soothing and simple and needed.

And so it's been in the year since she passed. Every time I miss my sis, another message saved for 100 days is waiting to bring comfort and a smile. How this could have been timed so perfectly, I will never know. But I do know that her messages are a gift; my voice mail from heaven.

Spirit, although I cannot feel you or see you or even hear your voice, my faith tells me you are there. Your presence brings me comfort, and I am grateful for that extra strength as I struggle to get through this situation. Thank you. Amen.

Come to me, all you that are weary and carrying heavy burdens, and I will give you rest. Take my yoke upon you, and learn from me; for I am gentle and humble in heart, and you will find rest for your souls. For my yoke is easy, and my burden is light.

Matthew 11:28–30

Be patient with sorrow, for it has its own lessons to teach. Do not rush to overcome grief, for it has many hidden gifts. Rather, let suffering swell and subside on its own, like the natural rhythm of the ocean waves upon the steadfast shore.

My Creator, I know in my heart that these tears will one day give way to joy, yet for now I know only pain. Help me to find the courage to let these tears flow, to feel the loss and heartbreak, so that I may come out whole and cleansed. For on the other side of my grief, I know life waits for me, and I know that my departed loved one would want me to live and laugh again.

GRIEF

When we lose something that we value we feel a little lost ourselves, don't we? Whether it's a friend moving away, a house fire that takes our belongings, or a dream dashed on the rocks, it hurts. Even if it's simply a realization that life doesn't always meet our expectations, it's tough to face.

The irony of loss is that we all feel it at one time or another, and yet when we're in the midst of it, we often feel alone. Know that you are not alone, no matter how lost or grief-stricken you may feel. In ancient times, grief was a very public thing. People dressed differently while in mourning. They cut their hair. They wore sackcloth and even adorned themselves with ashes. They behaved out of the ordinary. There were customs in place for dealing with grief.

But now we grieve in private. We leave each other alone, and it only increases our pain and isolation. Be brave enough to reach out. Find someone who can be com-

fortable being with you in your sadness.
Let yourself grieve whatever you have lost.
Grief isn't endless. It will run its course. It
just takes time.

**_Take comfort in God's promise that he will
never require more than you can give._**

*Father, before I was born you knew these
moments would come. Though it's hard to
believe right now, I know you wouldn't give
me more than I could bear. So help me dig
deep and find it within myself to face these
moments. Give me a sense of your presence.
Grant me the courage and the wisdom to take
the next few steps in the right direction.
Amen.*

THESE THINGS

Warm spring days, careless and inspired,
Cozy autumn nights, sitting by a fire,
Laughing till you cry,
Though you don't remember why,
Come morning.
Smiles from a friend at just the right time,
First infatuation, favorite valentine,
Holding someone tight,
Snuggled in at night,
Safe and warm.
Remember all these things when life gets
    cold,
Or turns on a dime, or makes you feel old,
Make yourself a list,
Know that you are missed,
And so loved.

Learning to comfort others is a gift.
Learning to comfort ourselves is a blessing.

With weeping they shall come, and with
consolations I will lead them back.

Jeremiah 31:9

If wisdom comes with experience, then
comfort comes from being wise enough to
know we can overcome any experience with
courage, faith, and integrity.

LOSING A FRIEND

The death of a loved one is a terrible and tragic event. But for Reese, her grief was coupled with the fact that her loved one was not human but canine. And Reese knew that most people thought mourning an animal so deeply was ridiculous.

Still, she could not deny the pain that flooded her heart and shattered her spirit. Toby had been her constant companion since she was 15. Now, 18 years later, she had been forced to say goodbye way too quickly. The cancer that ravaged her beloved dog had appeared suddenly and moved through his big, strong body with a speed that was shocking.

There would be no funeral or formal mourning, though. Reese's own family and friends didn't feel it was worth their time. Reese had been told over and over again to just "get over it" because "it was only a dog." Nobody understood that Toby had been so much more. He had been her best friend.

She decided to bury Toby in a beautiful pet cemetery near her house. She went by herself and made the arrangements, and on a warm and sunny Saturday afternoon, she watched as the two kind cemetery workers laid Toby into the ground in a white wooden casket. Then they left Reese alone to pray silently and mourn. She stayed there for at least an hour, feeling the hot sun on her back.

I will turn their mourning into joy, I will comfort them, and give them gladness for sorrow.

Jeremiah 31:13

As she knelt at the grave and cried, Reese sensed movement behind her. She turned to see a family of five standing there smiling at her. They introduced themselves as the Morans. They had just buried their family dog and wanted to offer their condolences to Reese. She smiled through her tears and got to her feet, taking their outstretched hands. She could feel the love and sincerity in their eyes.

As they talked, three more people came up and introduced themselves to Reese and offered their support. Before long, Reese was surrounded by two dozen people there to grieve their lost pets. She had never felt so comforted and understood. It broke her heart that her own family and friends were not there, but the people that surrounded her now, offering their unconditional love, proved to her that she was not alone in her love for her pet.

Just knowing there were others who shared her feelings filled her heart with a warmth that rivaled the sun.

God, your love for me is as strong as the sun and as comforting as a warm bath on a cold, dark night. Your presence assures me that even when I am suffering, there is joy waiting around the corner. Even as I feel alone, there are people who love and care for me if I open my heart and let them in. Amen.

By his strength,
Weakness is made strong,
By his generosity,
My life is full and blessed.
By his grace,
Sin is vanquished,
By his sacrifice,
Even such as I may be saved.

Those of steadfast mind you keep in peace—
in peace because they have trust in you.
Trust in the Lord forever, for in the Lord
God you have an everlasting rock.

Isaiah 26:3–4

Be still my soul: the Lord is on your side.
Bear patiently the cross of grief or pain;
leave to your God to order and provide; in
every change God faithful will remain.

Katherine von Schlegel

Sing for joy, O heavens, and exult, O Earth;
break forth O mountains, into singing!
For the Lord has comforted his people,
and will have compassion on his
suffering ones.

Isaiah 49:13

Life's struggles seem a whole lot easier when
you keep a supply of good friends on hand.

I HEAR YOU

Natasha's family prided itself on looking at the bright side. Feeling blue for no particular reason? "Well, no wonder you're blue," was their attitude. "You've been cooped up in the house all of this beautiful day. Get out of the house and get some fresh air!"

So intense was the unintentional pressure on Natasha to be happy, in fact, that as she grew up, she felt guilty on days when she was down. She chided herself that it was selfish to feel sad when she had so many blessings. Even when rocked by the inevitable mood swings of adolescence, Natasha was careful, at least outwardly, to "let a smile be her umbrella," as the family saying went.

When she became a young adult, Natasha's sunny disposition and ready smile attracted many friends. As her friends were beset with the heartbreaks of early adulthood—the breakups of love affairs, the sometimes fruitless searches for jobs—Natasha counseled them as she had always been counseled, to look on the bright side. She urged a friend whose flat, hollow voice on the phone long distance sounded dangerously despondent to count all the people who loved her and all the reasons she had to live. She urged a friend who lost her father to remember how many wonderful years she had enjoyed with him and how many children never knew their fathers at all. She encouraged a friend who broke an engagement to get right back out and start dating again: plenty of other fish in the sea.

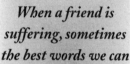

When a friend is suffering, sometimes the best words we can offer are spoken in the silence of just being there.

Natasha was so bent on being positive that it took her a long time to recognize the looks of frustration on her friends' faces when she gave such advice. She felt bad when she advised a friend who was depressed that things would look better in the morning, and the friend exploded angrily. "You don't get it! It's morning that I hate the worst. That's when I want to pull the covers over my head!"

As time went on, Natasha still had many friends, but it hurt to realize how few of them brought their troubles to her anymore. She didn't want to be a fair-weather friend. And then suddenly, for no reason that she could identify, Natasha's world turned a far darker color than the denim of ordinary blues. She had never experienced anything like it—the hope-lessness, the sorrow, the constant gray drizzle in her mind. She would have given anything to pull her socks up, to quit feel-ing sorry for herself, to snap out of it, as her well-intentioned family advised. How she cringed to hear her own bromides spoken back to her and to realize how unhelpful they were.

Instead it took medication, time, and the support of her friends to get better. During that dark time, Natasha found that the greatest comfort came from friends who affirmed her feelings rather than minimized her pain. She wasn't at all sure that this, too, would pass. In fact, she was terrified that she would always feel this terrible. So she learned to treasure the friends who said, "I hear you"; "That's really lousy"; "I'm so sorry you feel bad"; and "Talk to me." Most of all, she appreciated those who simply came, sat by her side, and held her hand.

After the fog of Natasha's depression lifted, she resolved to become a good listener herself. When those family members who had urged her to look on the bright side went through bad patches of their own, she gently tried to change the family pattern. She let them know that sometimes the only way to quit feeling rotten is to go ahead and let yourself feel rotten for a while. "That must be really tough," she would commiserate, or "I can see why you're sad."

Although Natasha's experience with depression had been a terrifying and humbling one, she was glad to have had it. If

she had never needed to be truly comforted in a time of extremity, she could
never have become a comforter herself.

*Heavenly Spirit, you alone provide the com-
fort that eases my heart when things are not
going well in my world. By leaning upon your
column of strength, I am able to move through
the darkness to where the light of hope shines
brightly. Thank you for always being there to
hold me, protect me, and love me when I am
scared. Amen.*

**Just being there for a friend in distress is
more comforting and encouraging than all
the self-help books and talk shows in the
world.**

NOTHING FANCY

A simple, caring gesture,
a gentle, loving touch,
fills the empty spaces of the soul.
A special gift of friendship,
a kind and thoughtful act
mends a broken heart and makes it whole.

*Lord, help me to provide comfort for a loved
one in need today. Help me to find just the
right thing to say and do that will make this
person feel better, even if it is only for a little
while. Make me an instrument of your peace,
your love, and your mercy. Amen.*

When it comes to comfort, it's hard to say who benefits more: the giver or the receiver.

If you want to be comforted, give comfort.

If you seek forgiveness, forgive.

If you need friendship, be a friend.

If you desire blessings to fill your life, be a blessing in someone else's.

God's love is chocolate for the soul, chicken soup for the spirit, and a soothing balm that comforts the body's aches and pains.

The Lord is good, a stronghold in a day of trouble; he protects those who take refuge in him, even in a rushing flood.

Nahum 1:7–8

In the deepest hour of grief

I can only find faith the size of a mustard
  seed to carry on.

I am afraid and alone and my strength has
  left me.

But then I remember God's promise to
  meet me halfway.

If I offer even the tiniest bit of faith unto
  him, he will take care of the rest.

And so I offer God my mustard seed. And
  he plants it for me.

And my faith grows.

Gifts of Grace

Therefore let us draw near with confidence to the throne of grace, so that we may receive mercy and find grace to help in time of need.

Hebrews 4:4

SMALL THINGS

Like the title of a favorite book she used to read to her now-grown children, Carmen was having a "no good, very bad day." She woke up grumpy. She got a run in a brand-new pair of control-top panty hose she had been saving for a fat mood (today was the day) the minute she put them on. She took one look in the mirror and decided that she was not only having a bad hair day but a bad hair life. She even picked a fight with her husband for leaving the bathroom messy, even though he'd left it no messier than usual. They parted for the day without their usual kiss.

Because she had left the house a little later than usual, Carmen hit the interstate at its morning traffic peak. Thoroughly prepared to wait in the lineup, be late to work, and get a raised eyebrow from her persnickety manager, she was so startled when another driver motioned her in that she almost forgot to give him a wave of gratitude.

> *So we do not lose heart . . . our inner nature is being renewed day by day.*
>
> 2 Corinthians 4:16

At work, one of her coworkers had anonymously left a little bag of her favorite candy in her mail slot. Having skipped breakfast and being in a "poor little me" mood, her choices were to eat them (not eating them was not a choice) and enjoy them or to berate herself for not having willpower. She chose the former.

The usual Monday morning staff meeting was held shortly thereafter. Carmen was prepared to shoulder more than her share of a group project and feel martyred as usual. But then a fresh-faced young coworker, a new hire, volunteered for some of the grunt work. Carmen had to smile in spite of herself. Wasn't anybody going to let her wallow in her bad day?

She guessed not. At lunchtime, she was coming back to work after a meal in a neighborhood café when she spotted a regular in the neighborhood. Smiley, a mentally challenged man who prowled the urban streets surrounding Carmen's office for cans and bottles, got his nickname because of his perpetual, radiant smile. Usually when Carmen saw Smiley coming, she crossed the street, as he had a habit of asking people to stop and pray with him. But today she smiled back at him and even let him take her hand in his big, grubby one as he led her in a quick and simple prayer of gratitude for the beautiful day the Lord had made.

After work, Carmen made a quick run to the grocery store. As she was leaving the parking lot, she was annoyed to find herself stuck behind an elderly woman who was driving very slowly. When the driver pulled up alongside the store's exit, her 80-something friend walked out of the store. The buddy tugged up one side of her skirt, gave her ankle a saucy twirl, and stuck out her thumb as if hitching a ride. Carmen cracked up in spite of herself.

On the way home, she mused that all day complete strangers had given her comfort, coaxing her out of her dark mood.

When she went in the door, she saw that her husband had built a fire. He was in the kitchen warming the chili she had made the night before. Tonight it was his turn to cook. Ordinarily, this would have struck Carmen as lazy. But when he looked up, gauging her mood and asking if chili sounded good, she answered, "Sure. It's always better the next day."

As they ate in front of the fire, Carmen told him of her experience with Smiley. She concluded rather wistfully, "Why is it that when you see an adult with a perpetual happy smile you know there's something wrong?"

Her husband answered, "There's nothing wrong. They smile because they're the only ones who know the secret."

"What's that?" Carmen asked.

"That the best things in life aren't things."

God, my day is so hectic, and I barely have time to take care of myself. I am feeling stressed, alone, and resentful toward others for not helping me out more. Please bring me some small comfort today to make it just a little easier. With a good night's sleep, I know I'll feel stronger tomorrow. Amen.

IN MY SHOES

When I'm feeling anxious
and the world seems insane,
and the TV noise is giving
my poor head a searing pain,
I'll go outside and take a stroll
and breathe in cool, fresh air
and let my mind drift upward
to float without a care.
Because sometimes nothing does the trick
like walking off your blues
and being out in nature in
a pair of comfy shoes.

*Live purely in the moment, and you'll have
a day you can cherish forever.*

The best cure for earthly cares is to look at the world through the eyes of a child:

There are no mountains in the way—only hills to climb.

There are no bills to pay—only quarters for ice cream.

There are no faces of strangers—only friends they haven't met yet.

There is no crime, contention, or war—only squabbles forgotten about tomorrow.

There is no future to worry about—only an afternoon of endless possibilities.

To a little child, there is nothing that milk and cookies, a nap, or a hug won't fix.

A LITTLE FRIENDSHIP

Sitting in the crowded hospital waiting room, Laura had the distinct feeling that someone was watching her. But nobody seemed to be looking her way. Maybe the stress was getting to her. Laura's best friend had been in a terrible auto accident, and she was waiting for word on her status.

Her friend Sandy had been in the passenger seat of a van full of women on their way to a Moms' Night Out event where mothers get to take a break and have an evening without husbands or kids. Apparently, the van had been cut off by a semi and veered off the road, tumbling twice before coming to rest in a ditch.

Laura had been planning to go with them but had begged off at the last second with an oncoming cold. She had felt strange going anyway, since Sandy was the only other mom she knew. Now, she felt a strong wave of guilt wash over her, especially when she learned that two of the other moms in the van had died at the scene.

Sandy was in the ICU, undergoing surgery. She had been unconscious when Laura got to the hospital, and Sandy's husband, Jim, said there was internal bleeding. All they could do was wait. Jim was sitting with Sandy's family, but Laura had wanted to sit by herself and process the events of the night. She couldn't stop thinking that had she joined the moms' night outing, she might not be alive right now.

Every generous act of giving, with every perfect gift, is from above, coming down from the Father of lights.

James 1:17

As she sat and prayed quietly for Sandy to be okay, Laura again felt as though somebody's eyes were on her. She turned, and the only person that seemed to be looking her way was a small boy of about six or seven holding a large teddy bear. The little boy smiled at her, and she forced herself to smile back.

Laura turned back to her own thoughts, now wondering who the boy was. He was not with Sandy's family. She wondered what terrible fate he was waiting to hear. She hoped it wasn't too bad, but her thoughts were again interrupted when Sandy's surgeon motioned for Jim.

As Jim talked with the surgeon, Laura watched Jim's face. He looked crestfallen, and Laura felt a lump in her throat. She wanted to sit with the family now, but when she got up, something made her stumble. She looked down and saw the large teddy bear the little boy had been holding. On it was a piece of white paper and a message scrawled in crayon, "Here is a friend for you."

Laura looked for the boy, but he was nowhere in sight. She asked the attending nurses at the desk if they had seen him. One of the nurses said the boy and his family had gone home, having heard the good news that the boy's aunt was resting comfortably after her surgery.

Laura felt dizzy. She was grateful that the boy's aunt was doing well, but there was still Sandy to worry about.

Holding the bear close, she walked over to Jim and gave him a hug. He smiled through his tears and shared the news. Sandy was almost out of surgery, and it appeared she was going to be okay. It would be a long road, and she would need all the friends she could get.

Laura smiled and handed the teddy bear to Jim, asking that he give it to Sandy as soon as he could. Then she sat down with the family and waited.

May God give you of heaven's dew and of earth's richness.

Genesis 27:28 NIV

Lord, let not the small blessings of each day pass us by, even when our eyes are too filled with tears to see them. Remind us that kindness, caring, and friendship are everywhere when we stay alert and awake to the good things in life. Although we may be afraid, let us always remember that we are never alone and that love truly conquers all. Amen.

Even in my grief, I am aware of a loving presence that is ever available to me. In the arms of God I can find the rest that my weary soul needs and the comfort that will soothe my aching heart.

Take comfort in the little things:
Giggling with children
Playing cards with an old friend
Walking in the rain
Swinging as high as you can
Writing a letter
Taking a bubble bath
Petting a kitten
Eating chocolate
Watching the sunrise
Singing yourself a love song.

The grass withers, the flower fades; but the word of our God will stand forever.

Isaiah 40:8

GLORIOUSLY AVERAGE

It was a Friday night, and Mary was discouraged as she trudged to her car through the slush of the parking lot. That day, she had received her annual performance review. "Meets expectations," she'd been told. "Solid." "Dependable." Just good enough to get the usual cost-of-living raise. She knew what that meant: She was average. Back in grade school, she'd been in the "blue" reading group, which—average or not—she was smart enough to know meant right smack dab in the middle. She'd followed the same unspectacular course in high school, taking classes in what was called the "general track." Like her fellow classmates, who grew up to become mechanics and beauticians, she knew that teachers didn't expect kids in the general track to set the world on fire.

When she got home, Mary called one of the women in the group of friends she met every Friday evening for dinner and a movie, begging off with a headache. Her friend was astonished: Mary, never ill, was as constant as the moon. Mary sighed when she got off the phone. Her Friday nights were fun but, like her life, predictable. And while she was grateful for her friends, she wished just once they'd praise her for her imagination, style, or outrageous wit instead of her common sense.

God puts something good and wonderful in every [person] His hands create.

Mark Twain

The next day Mary was in too restless a mood to follow her usual Saturday inclinations: a long walk with her dog (a mutt of no particular distinction, of course), perhaps a little gardening, a nice lunch out with a friend, maybe a trip to the library. Instead she puttered around her house, frowning at herself in the mirror, finding fault with her conventional beige carpet, and flinging open the door of her carefully organized closet to survey its neatly pressed khakis and medium-quality blazers in disgust.

The next day something compelled Mary to go to church even though she wasn't in the mood. At first, she was disappointed to learn that the pastor, a compelling speaker, was ill. Filling in was the assistant pastor, Ruth, a plain, graying middle-age woman with a hesitant, tremulous voice. As Ruth began to speak, Mary had to suppress a yawn.

Soon, though, Ruth's voice gathered strength, and Mary began to listen. Ruth was talking about "ordinary time," the time in the church calendar between the big spectacular holidays when nothing much goes on. Ruth talked about how much she loved ordinary time—quiet time with her grandchildren spent cooking, reading aloud, or even just watching TV. Ruth said that if she could relive any day of her life, it would be an ordinary Saturday when she was a kid, helping her dad with farm chores and going in at dusk. Her mom would open the door for them,

Ruth said, and the house would smell of apple pie.

After church, Mary began thinking of her ordinary time. She thought about how her siblings always teased her because whatever else was on her menu, she always also made a plain old box of macaroni and cheese when they came for dinner, in case her nephews and nieces didn't like the main course. She thought about how she called her widowed father every Sunday. She thought about how she sang in a community choir and, though never offered a solo, was always on time and prepared. She thought about work, where she seldom initiated new ideas but almost never took sick leave and was often the first to arrive and the last to leave.

Suddenly, Mary felt comforted. She felt enough like her usual self to go to a funky neighborhood filled with secondhand stores to stroll and browse. Catching sight of herself in a plate glass window, she saw an average-looking woman with light brown hair—nobody you'd look at twice

were it not for the lightness in her step.
Yes, she was ordinary. How extraordinary
that was!

*God of all comfort, I feel small and helpless
today, like a child in need of a strong and
loving hug. Let me turn to you for the gentle,
yet powerful reassurance that will bring me
fresh hope and newfound faith so that I can
once again live my life with maturity, grace,
and inner peace. Amen.*

**I have indeed received much joy and
encouragement from your love.**

Philemon 1:7 NIV

Like stars in the sky or grains of sand,
His creations are immeasurable.
Yet, he says, "I know you.
Even the very hairs on your
head are numbered."
Inconceivable as it may be,
We are all unique and familiar
To the Father who created us all.

The human mind plans the way, but the
Lord directs the steps.

Proverbs 16:9

You're Never Too Old
for a Security Blanket

As an investment banker with a generous income, Renata had plenty of money for decorating her sophisticated new loft apartment. What she didn't have was a good eye. Although she could spot a promising investment miles away, she didn't have the gift for creating an appealing look at home. So she asked for the help of her decorator friend Annie. With Annie's assistance, she established a contemporary look with textured paints, linen pillows, and a leather couch, all in subtly varying shades of white and off-white: vanilla, eggshell, ivory, and sand. Her friends oohed and aahed when they came to visit.

And yet Renata had one favorite thing that she hadn't shown Annie because she suspected that it didn't go at all: a quilt her grandmother had made during the Depression. A heavy thing, the quilt was fashioned out of outgrown and worn-out "Sunday go to meeting" suits as well as everyday over-coats and jackets that Renata's father, uncles, and grandfathers had used to warm themselves, collars turned up against the unforgiving wind, on the flat and treeless plains of Nebraska. When Renata stretched out under the quilt, she could just hear her grandmother saying, "Use it up, wear it out, make it do, or do without."

The squares were made of sturdy wool and corduroy coats that had been ordered from the Sears catalog. The family lived in remote small towns too far from Omaha or Lincoln to go there to shop. What an occasion it was, her grandmother had told her with sparkling eyes, when a package arrived from Sears!

Love is a big, soft comforter you can wrap your trembling heart in.

On winter nights when her all-white, high-ceilinged apartment felt sterile and drafty, Renata liked to gather the quilt close around her. She would explore with a lazy forefinger the textures of the fabric: the warp of a brown corduroy that must have felt good on bitter nights, the roughness of a gray tweed. The underside was a soft gray flannel that had probably also been used for pajamas, thinned from years of use. The quilt was her version of a child's security blanket. She wrapped herself in its homey warmth whenever she was tired, anxious, or ill or when, as an urban professional living far from extended family, she simply needed the solace of home.

Each of the top pieces of the quilt was tied in with a single tassel of bright orange yarn. That made Renata smile. Because Renata's grandfather was a depot agent for the railroad, her father had grown up in apartments over train stations. She could just see her grandmother tying off those tassels, attempting with her darning needle to make something gay and pretty out of the drab leftover fabrics as the desolate prairie wind howled around the depot. How she must have longed to go to the city and splurge on sunny stripes and bright floral prints!

One of the things Renata liked best about the quilt was the slight rustling sound it made when she smoothed it down. Once she had peeked inside a small frayed place on the underside and found that it was stuffed with newspapers. That would have made sense during the Depression; batting cost money, yesterday's news was free.

One night a few weeks after she moved into her new apartment, Renata was warding off an oncoming cold with a cup of tea and a handful of vitamin C tablets as she burrowed under the quilt, its softness draped over the angular arms of her cold leather couch. The doorbell rang. It was her decorator friend Annie, who had found herself in the neighborhood and stopped by to admire the way the apartment had come together with her unique touch.

"Renata!" she cried as she came in. "Where on earth did you get that quilt?

It's so funky! The contrast with the white makes it perfect in here."

Renata was astonished and pleased, sheepishly confessing that she'd had it forever but hadn't shown it to Annie because she thought it would look hopelessly out of place in her stylish new digs. Renata shared the story of the quilt with Annie over a cup of tea. After her friend left, Renata realized that while she might never develop an eye for decorating, from now on she would understand that the comfort of a humble hand-worked item made with love is never out of style.

Spirit, carry me like a feather upon the river to a place of serenity. Let the waters flow over me like cleansing balm, washing away my grief. Set me upon the dry place, where life begins anew. Amen.

God of all comfort, only you can provide the security I seek amid life's unexpected storms. Be my constant companion, always caring, always there to guide me. No longer will I seek comfort from outside but always from your presence deep within my soul. Thank you, God. Amen.

The wind blows where it chooses, and you hear the sound of it, but you do not know where it comes from or where it goes. So it is with everyone who is born of the Spirit.

John 3:8

PLACES AND PEOPLE

What was the safest place you ever knew? Was it somewhere in your childhood? Was it associated with someone special? Can you go there for a moment of respite when the waves get a little too high in life's seas? Who is the safest person you ever knew? Did they hug you tight? Did they make you laugh? Were they always there when you needed them?

All these good things come our way to make us strong. They weave into our fabric and offer us resilience. They teach us that life has its pockets of goodness to balance the pockets of insanity. It is important that we know how to access our safe places and safe people even in the difficulties of life.

The safest places and the safest people you ever knew are still accessible to you through your memories and maybe even through a phone call. Don't leave them behind at any cost. They are gifts for a lifetime.

*To everything there is a season, and a time
to every purpose under the heaven.*

Ecclesiastes 3:1

*Lord, bring me to the place where peace flows
like a river, where soft green grasses gently
hold the weight of my tired body, where the
light of a new sun casts warmth to melt the
coldness of my heart. Lord, have mercy upon
my grieving soul, and guide me to the well of
sweet healing waters, that I may drink and
know joy once again.*

I will lift up my eyes unto the hills, from whence will come my help.

My help cometh from the Lord, which made heaven and earth.

He will not suffer thy foot to be moved; he that keepeth thee will not slumber.

The Lord is thy keeper: the Lord is thy shade upon thy right hand.

The sun shall not smite thee by day, nor the moon by night.

The Lord shall preserve thee from all evil: he shall preserve thy soul.

The Lord shall preserve thy going out and thy coming in from this time forth, and even for evermore.

Psalm 121:18

The Lord will guide you continually and you shall be like a watered garden, like a spring of water, whose waters never fail.

Isaiah 58:11

Consider it all joy, my brethren, when you encounter various trials, knowing that the testing of your faith produces endurance. And let endurance have its perfect result, so that you may be perfect and complete, lacking in nothing.

James 1:2–4

Lift Up Your Heart

Rejoice in the Lord always; again I will say, Rejoice. Let your gentleness be known to everyone. The Lord is near. Do not worry about anything, but in everything by prayer and supplication with thanksgiving let your requests be made known to God. And the peace of God, which surpasses all understanding, will guard your hearts and your minds in Christ Jesus.

Philippians 4:4–7

SMALL PLANET

When Allen gradually began to close his pet store, Small Planet, it was a big event in his close-knit town. The store was a kid-friendly place with big floor pillows to plunk down on, a three-legged rabbit to pet, an abused dog that Allen had rescued from the pound and taught to do tricks, and a giant turtle called Mr. Slow. Small Planet was Allen's life. He organized story hours on Saturday mornings, cat and dog shows throughout the year, dog training sessions, and a pet-owner costume contest on Halloween.

When he became ill, there were days—especially chemo days—when it was all he and his assistant could do to care for the animals. He just wasn't up to opening the store. He hated the unpredictability of that for his loyal customers, hated to think of little kids with their noses pressed against the plate glass, looking longingly in at the puppies.

And so, using his customer mailing list, he wrote this letter to the parents of the

children who frequented his shop:
"Dear Friends,

You may have noticed that Small Planet has been closed a good deal of the time lately, and I apologize if that has been frustrating for you. You and your children may have also noticed that I don't quite seem myself lately. I am writing to help you talk to your children about what is happening to me and the store, if that is something you would like to do.

I have cancer. It started in my lungs and has spread to my bones. Oddly enough, I have never smoked. I can't help thinking that the high rates of cancer have to do with something that is in our soil or our air. We should take better care of our small planet, shouldn't we?

By the way, I don't think of myself as 'battling cancer' but living with it. As you know, I love nature in all of its grandness and mystery. I have looked at my own metastasized cells under a microscope. They are rather beautiful and awesome in the sheer force and speed with which they multiply. My hope is that some day perhaps one of your children, working with nature, will help find a way to slow such cells down.

I still have a good quality of life and will open the store whenever I can. Please don't try to hush your children when they ask why I'm wearing that big Dr. Seuss hat all the time now, why I breathe funny, or why I can't talk loudly enough to read the stories to them myself at

But the land that you are crossing over to occupy is a land of hills and valleys, watered by rain from the sky, a land that the Lord your God looks after.

Deuteronomy 11:11

Story Time. Unlike adults who sometimes look away and say nothing, their stares and innocent questions are a breath of fresh air.

I have loved getting to know you and your children. I have tried to live my values through small things like using recycled bags in the shop and telling the kids why. I

have loved seeing new worlds of knowl-
edge open to them and watching the joy
and sense of responsibility they develop
when they care for a pet.

I want to live as long as I can, but I do
not fear death. When the time comes for
me to go, it may comfort your children to
know that I believe I will become part of
our small planet, part of the wind, part of
the earth, part of the trees. I am glad to
talk to them about all of this when they
are in the store. In fact, I have found that
comforting them is a comfort to me.

Sincerely,

Allen Havelock."

Allen died three months after he wrote
the letter. The memorial service was held
outside, in the little city park across the
street from Small Planet. It was a good
thing—there were so many parents and
children there that a church would have
barely contained them.

Father, please take care of my friends. Give them the comfort of your love. Remind them of the comfort of my love. Help them not to feel alone. Help them instead to see the arms of their community around them. Amen.

GOD'S BLESSINGS

God's grace is as deep as the ocean,
God's love is as wide as the endless blue
   sky,
God's wisdom is as bright as a million suns,
God's strength is as strong as the mountains are high.

Thus says the Lord:
Stand at the crossroads, and look, and ask for
the ancient paths, where the good way lies;
and walk in it, and find rest for your souls.

Jeremiah 6:16

If you are pure and upright, surely then he
will rouse himself for you and restore you to
your rightful place. Though your beginning
was small, your latter days will be
very great.

Job 8:6–7

Love is from God; everyone who loves is
born of God and knows God.

1 John 4:7

SWEETENING THE DAY

The emergency room at a large hospital is not only a busy place, it's also a stressful one. Emergency room physician Dr. Dan tried to keep things light to help his staff relax. He bombarded them with treats, jokes, and funny stories. He popped fist-fuls of candy-coated chocolates and shared his secret stash with his colleagues. His exuberance kept his team from much of the usual stress and burnout experienced by emergency workers.

Dr. Dan himself was a tireless worker, often taking double shifts at the hospital to fill in when others were ill or on vaca-tion. He always had his candy with him to sweeten the day.

An ardent angler, the young doctor liked to fly to exotic locations all over the world in search of that special fishing hole. On his last trip, Dr. Dan had an accident and died, doing the thing he loved best, fishing. His wife and colleagues refused to give in to sadness, so instead of a funeral service, there was a celebration of his life.

Everyone told "Dr. Dan" stories, and songs and prayers were offered to give him a good sendoff. At the end of the celebration, amid much ceremony, his medical team from the hospital carried in a huge glass container. They set it on a table near the door, then snapped off the cloth cover to reveal thousands of colorful candy-coated chocolates.

Only God can turn our mourning into dancing; our sorrow into joy.

Tears flowed as each guest filed out with a fistful of the brightly colored candies—comfort food—to sweeten the sorrow as they faced life without their good friend and colleague.

Look to the source in any thing, and be comforted in every thing.

Lord, continue to shower your blessings on those who team with you to bring comfort to the afflicted. When their caring hearts grow weary, touch them. Strengthen them for the work ahead and give them your peace. Amen.

The comforts of the world are fleeting,
Happiness but a moment;
Pleasures that fade beneath the light of
   day.
But God's peace is everlasting,
And his blessings infinite;
Our reward, in him, eternal.

*Are you weary, persecuted, in mourning,
burdened with cares? God will comfort you
and trade your sorrows for a happy heart.*

*Dear Spirit, I look to you for my soul's
renewal. In faith and hope I seek shelter from
the storms of despair that may come in the
days ahead. In strength and courage I seek the
power to mourn my loss and begin the healing
that will one day make me whole and new
again. Walk with me, Spirit, walk beside me
and hold my hand and together we will face
this loss with hope.*

JUST LIKE ME

Teri had always known she was adopted. She grew up with the notion that she was "chosen" and "special." Yet there was a restless longing hidden beneath her sunny smile.

At first, she enjoyed a happy childhood as an only child. Her father took her horseback riding and skiing and spent happy days with her, hiking in the woods and boating along the New England coast. Then came his promotion and, along with that, incessant traveling and weeks at a time away from the family.

Surely goodness and mercy will follow me all the days of my life, and I will dwell in the house of the Lord forever.

Psalm 23:6 NIV

Loneliness became a permanent member of the household. Then her mother became ill, and her grandmother came to take care of her.

Because she spent so much time in the company of adults, Teri had little time to be a child and plenty of time to wonder, *Who am I? Where did I come from?* But she was too loyal to the people she knew as her parents to question aloud.

The little girl grew up, and one by one, her parents and grandmother died. But her desire to learn about her roots remained alive. An ache welled up in her, a deep longing to be comforted by someone who loved her.

When the last member of her adoptive family died, Teri contacted a lawyer, who learned that her birth mother's identity was confidential. He agreed to contact her to see if she wanted to meet Teri. At first, the mother was reluctant because the child was not her husband's.

But Teri was determined to meet her mother no matter what the answer. *Even if I have to appear at her doorstep disguised as a delivery person,* she thought.

Finally, with her husband's permission, Teri's birth mother agreed to meet with her at a restaurant halfway between their towns. Teri arrived early, full of excitement. Soon the awful ache would be gone—that void inside her would be filled. She wondered if she would recognize her mother. *Maybe she won't like me,* Teri thought, suddenly panicky. "Maybe she'll hate me."

Her eyes scanning the parking lot, Teri focused on a tall, attractive woman with red hair the same shade as her own. Their eyes locked, and Teri took in a quick breath. *She looks just like me,* Teri realized. Instinctively, the two women started to move toward each other.

Soon they were in each other's arms, laughing and comparing their bony knees and feet, high arches, sprinkling of freckles across their noses, long slender fingers, and crinkling blue eyes that disappeared when they smiled.

They were nearly identical—right down to the huge empty place in their hearts— the space that was now comfortably filled for both of them.

God of all comfort, we give you praise. You come to us in our need and cover us with your love. You lift our fallen heads and breathe new life into us. You fill the empty spaces in our hearts so we can feel whole again. Thank you, Lord. Amen.

No Prescription Required

Comfort requires no payment.
Cuddles and prayers are free.
To find that we're loved and cared for,
Is the best medicine there could be.

Gracious is the Lord and righteous; our God is merciful. The Lord protects the simple; when I was brought low, he saved me. Return, O my soul, to your rest, for the Lord has dealt bountifully with you.

Psalm 116:5–7

God's comfort is available for the asking, and his peace is free of charge.

THE LANGUAGE OF LOVE

Excitement bubbled within Sara as she arrived in the Mexican village to the greetings of smiling children with lively dark eyes. She had joined her classmates on a spring-break service project to build a school in this dusty mountain town.

During the orientation meeting, Sara could hear the children playing and laughing outdoors as they waited for the student volunteers to join them in their play. But when the enthusiastic students stepped out into the sunshine, they were confronted by the sober face of their leader, who brought stunning news. A carload of their fellow students, headed for another service project, had been hit head-on by a drunk driver. All were killed.

Dealing with grief was never easy, but far from home, amidst a foreign culture, the task was overwhelming. Sara cried until she couldn't cry any more. Visions of her friends haunted her. Having answered God's call to serve the poor, she could no longer hear his voice at all.

As she headed to her sleeping quarters, Sara was intercepted by two little girls who threw their arms around her waist and hugged her tightly. They talked rapidly in Spanish. Neither the girls nor the student volunteers knew the others' language, and the barrier seemed insurmountable to Sara, who longed to hear words of comfort.

Sara had never felt so isolated in all her life. She started weeping again, but this time a tiny hand

Two are better than one . . . For if they fall, one will lift up the other.

Ecclesiastes 4:9–10

reached up to brush away her tears. Touched by this show of tenderness, Sara knelt down and embraced the children. With their simple acts, all barriers came crashing down. They were no longer strangers but members of a common humanity.

It didn't matter that they lacked a common language. When words failed, the girls had reached out to her in the universal language of love.

On that day, God spoke to Sara through little arms that hugged and tiny fingers that wiped her tears away.

You came to me, O Lord, and heard the outcry of my heart. I longed for comfort, and with the touch of a child's hand, you soothed my sorrow and healed my wounds. Help me gather the strength to go on, so I might touch others with the sweetness of your love and caring. Amen.

Often, our real blessings appear to us in the form of pains, losses, and disappointments; but through faith, patience, and hindsight, their true nature is revealed.

The Lord went in front of them in a pillar of cloud by day, to lead them along the way, and in a pillar of fire by night, to give them light, so that they might travel by day and by night. Neither the pillar of cloud by day nor the pillar of fire by night left its place in front of the people.

Exodus 13:21–22

God sews for me a patchwork quilt
A comforter from above;
He drapes it around my shoulders
And covers me with love.

Tap into the overflowing wellspring of wisdom deep within, and find all the comfort your thirsty spirit desires.

Lord, even when we pass through the toughest places of our lives, you are there with us. You see to it that though we walk through fire and flood, we are not overcome. You turn our weakness into strength so we can serve and praise you as we should. Amen.

Contributors

Marie D. Jones is an ordained minister and is widely published in books and magazines. She has contributed to *Mother's Daily Prayer Book, Bless This Marriage,* and *Simple Wisdom.*

Anne Broyles is a co-pastor who leads retreats on a variety of topics, such as family and women's spirituality. She is the author of a number of articles and books, including *Meeting God Through Worship* and *Journaling: A Spirit Journey.*

Rebecca Christian is a columnist and freelance writer who has written for *The Episcopalian* and National Catholic News Service. She contributed to *Heartwarmers: Grandmas Always Have Time* and *Heartwarmers: Moms Are the Best.*

June Eaton is a writer and teacher who has published stories and articles in more than 50 Christian publications. She has also contributed to several books, including *Heartwarmers: Moms Are the Best* and *Charming Expressions: Angels.*

Susan Farr Fahncke is a freelance writer whose work regularly appears in *Whispers from Heaven* magazine. She contributed to *An Angel by Your Side* and the *Stories from the Heart* series.

Carol Smith is an inspirational writer with an M.A. in religious education. She has contributed to several religious books, including *Angels Watching Over Us* and *Angels: Heavenly Blessings.*

Natalie Walker Whitlock is a freelance writer whose work has appeared in *Family Fun* and *Woman's Day* magazines. She was coauthor of *Silver Linings: Friends* and a contributor to *Angels Watching Over Us.*

Acknowledgments

Publications International, Ltd., has made every effort to locate the owners of all copyrighted material to obtain permission to use the selections that appear in this book. Any errors or omissions are unintentional; corrections, if necessary, will be made in future editions.

Unless otherwise noted, all Scripture quotations are taken from the *New Revised Standard Version* of the Bible. Copyright © 1989 by the Division of Christian Education of the National Council of the Churches of Christ in the United States of America. Used by permission. All rights reserved.

Scripture quotations marked NASB are taken from *The Holy Bible, New American Standard* version. Copyright © 1977, Holman Bible Publishers. All rights reserved.

Scripture quotations marked NIV are taken from *The Holy Bible, New International Version.* Copyright © 1973, 1978, 1984, International Bible Society. Used by permission of Zondervan Publishing House. All rights reserved.

Scripture quotations marked TLB are taken from *The Living Bible.* Copyright © 1971. Used by permission of Tyndale House Publishers, Inc. All rights reserved.

Scripture quotations marked KJV are taken from *The Holy Bible, King James Version.*